SUPER STRATEGIES

FOR

Everyday Teaching

 Anne M. Beninghof

www.IdeasForEducators.com

ISBN: 978-1-97466-386-6

Praise for *Super Strategies for Everyday Teaching*

"I love having a resource I can turn to that has so many tested, practical, engaging ideas to help learners of varying abilities."

—Alicia Osborn, Classroom Teacher

"Anne Beninghof has the ability to distill challenging topics down to simple decisions so that instead of feeling overwhelmed, teachers feel like they have a game plan to accomplish challenging tasks. When it comes to making implementable change, Super Strategies is a place to start if you really want results."

—Jethro Jones, Host of Transformative Principal Podcast, Transformative Leadership Summit, and 2017 National Digital Principal of the Year

"As a building principal I am always looking for ways to help teachers be more effective. Anne's teaching strategies hook the interest of our students, are easily applied by our teachers and give everyone a great feeling of success."

—Chris Trujillo, Principal

"Busy teachers will find these strategies easy to use, and effective for student engagement and increasing understanding of content material. I have used many of them and the ideas are especially helpful for students who struggle."

—Grace Helgeson, Teacher

"Anne Beninghof has developed and shared practical strategies that arm teachers with tools and resources to engage ALL students! They are simple, inexpensive instructional approaches that close the learning gap for even our most struggling learners. This new book will be an amazing, must have, resource for all teachers."

—Toni Palmer, Chief Leadership and Development Officer

Contents

Contents

Contents

Introduction

"Faster than a speeding bullet. More powerful than a locomotive. Able to leap tall buildings in a single bound. Look! Up in the sky! It's a bird. It's a plane. It's _____!"

— from *Adventures of Superman* (1952–1958)

I'm betting that every one of you can complete this sentence. One of the most iconic characters in television, movie and comic book history was Superman. As a child, I would rush into my house from school, quickly change into play clothes, and huddle in front of the television with my three brothers. My mother allowed us to watch Superman before digging into our homework assignments and chores. Perhaps she had a keen sense of how empowering superheroes are for children.

The best teachers are superheroes for their students every day. While we may not be able to leap tall buildings, we have other amazing super powers. Here are just a few:

X-Ray Vision

Thirty students in a class doesn't faze you—you can still see each one of them as the unique individuals they are. You take the time to notice when their personality changes, to see if their lunch box is empty, and to envision the best future possible for them.

Flexibility

Surprise! The principal wants to bring visitors to your classroom next period. No problem. A parent emails you to announce that she is running twenty minutes late for her after-school conference. No problem. You're super flexible.

Precognition

Children pulling pranks on each other—not in your class. You've seen it all before and take steps to stop unruly behavior before it ever starts. Your students think "How did she know?!?"

Force Field

A protective bubble encases your room so that children feel safe. You know the importance of brain safety for learning. Students are encouraged to take risks and participate because bullying, belittling and negative mindset have been vanquished in your class.

Juggling

Three balls? Four? Five? The sky's the limit for super teachers. You juggle relationships, individual student needs, state standards, evaluation systems, changing curricula—the list goes on and on. But so do you!

The best teachers accomplish amazing feats because they have an enormous cache of super strategies. They know the power of novelty to increase student attention, the power of multi-sensory activities to increase memory and the power of variety to allow for differing readiness levels and interests. *Super Strategies for Everyday Teaching* is filled with dozens of powerful ideas that are novel, multi-sensory and have proven to engage even the most reluctant child.

For more than thirty years I have been building a collection of super strategies that work for students of all kind—but especially those that struggle with engagement and understanding. These are the students who most need their teacher to be a superhero! I have always embraced the opportunity to work with these students, finding creative ideas to help them with the learning process. Not only do I love collecting new ideas, I also love sharing them with teachers around the world. I began doing that when I wrote my first book on inclusive practices. The response was so positive that I continued writing books and began sharing ideas through professional learning workshops. When the Internet arrived, I was ready with a website and blog posts, and have recently added webinars to the many methods I use to share great teaching strategies.

This collection of strategies now spans more than three decades of teaching experience. In *Super Strategies for Everyday Teaching* I've included the most practical and effective ideas because I know that teachers need things that work, but don't require much work. I love ideas that are simple enough to use the very next day! Whenever possible, I have included links to supporting materials so that you can download them to your own devices, as well as reproducibles for making copies. I believe you will find this collection something you can flip through quickly, find an appealing idea, dog-ear the page, and use it immediately.

Although I work as a consultant and coach all over the world, I am lucky enough to still be planning lessons and teaching children. To organize my favorite strategies, I create for myself an "Instructional Strategy Anchor Chart" (see following page). (Students need anchor charts as a quick reminder—why not teachers?) This tool serves as a visual reference—a cheat sheet—of my favorite instructional strategies. If I am teaching a lesson that isn't going as well as I had hoped, I can quickly refer to my anchor chart and make a change. Or, if I am bogged down in lesson planning and need some inspiration, I glance at my anchor chart for a relevant idea. As you begin trying the strategies from this book, record your favorites on your own anchor chart and store it somewhere handy.

In the back of the book I have added a few Notes pages so that you can capture the powerful ideas you have created. With all of these Super Strategies at your fingertips, you are sure to save the world, one child and one day at a time.

For digital versions of the reproducibles in this book,
go to https://tinyurl.com/yx52trth.

The reproducibles can also be found
on Anne's website at
www.ideasforeducators.com/downloadables.html.

Instructional Strategy Chart

Strategy	Page #	Purpose (when to use it)

Section

1

SenseAble Strategies

Super Strategies from the author's book, *SenseAble Strategies: Including Diverse Learners Through Multisensory Strategies* © 1998.

Featured Strategies:

1. High Contrast Backgrounds
2. Standing Work Stations
3. Magic Covers
4. Highlighting Tape

High Contrast Backgrounds

Off-task behavior is a common problem in classrooms, especially when students are expected to do book or paperwork at their desks. While there are many factors that can lead to off-task behavior, one factor is learning style. Visual learners may be distracted by classroom noises or by the wide array of posters and visual materials around them. Students who are predominately tactile, kinesthetic, or auditory learners are frequently challenged by the need to visually attend to paperwork. High Contrast Backgrounds provide extra visual stimulus to draw attention to the work area, often resulting in an increase in on-task behavior.

How To

1. Obtain large sheets (approximately 12 x 18 inches) of black and neon colored paper. Black and neon papers provide a High Contrast Background to books and work papers. Some students have more success with black, others with the neon colors.

2. Ask students to cover their desks or work surfaces with the High Contrast Background paper.

3. Monitor students' ability to focus on their work and have students switch high contrast papers until optimum performance is attained.

More Ideas

⮑ Cut 2-inch-wide strips of High Contrast Background paper and tape them around the top edges of the desk. This provides a simple outline for students who may be overwhelmed by a cover over their entire desks.

⮑ Neon masking tape (available at many hardware and office supply stores) can be used instead of paper to outline the desk.

Standing Workstations

Doctors tell us that when we are sitting, over two-thirds of our body weight rests on our lumbar region. While some students can tolerate this easily, many have difficulty staying in a sitting posture for any length of time. Kinesthetic learners usually leap at the chance to be out of their seats and move around. They actually *need* movement to *learn*. These are compelling reasons to consider implementing Standing Workstations.

How To

1. Prepare an area in the classroom for Standing Workstations. Effective Standing Workstations provide hard, sturdy work surfaces at the appropriate height for students. If preparing more than one Standing Workstation, consider making them slightly different heights to accommodate more students. Workstations can be made from:
   - Ironing boards (adjustable in height!)
   - Drafting or architectural tables
   - Media or utility carts
   - Tops of a freestanding bookcases
   - Counter tops
   - Varnished plywood or Formica can also be attached to a wall to fold up or out as needed

2. Determine rules for Standing Workstation behavior and communicate these clearly to students. Rules may need to address: wandering; talking; staying on task; and when, how, and by whom Workstations may be accessed.

3. Throughout the day direct students, especially kinesthetic learners, to go to a Standing Workstation. At the Workstation students may stand while they listen to a lecture, view a DVD, complete a worksheet, or read a book.

More Ideas

⮌ Students generally perform very well at Standing Workstations, but sometimes wander a bit too far from the designated area. To correct this, outline a standing area on the floor with masking tape. Make it clear to students that they must stay within the lines or return to their seats.

Magic Covers

Reading a text or storybook is often challenging for tactile learners and struggling readers. As a result, during "book time" students may become inattentive, frustrated, fidgety, or disruptive. Magic Covers are wonderful tools for decreasing these problems and for increasing student interaction with texts. Magic Covers are clear acetate report covers which can be placed over pages in a book. Teachers and students can then use colored markers to mark on the cover, as if they were marking in the book.

How To

1. Acquire clear acetate report covers or page protectors (Magic Covers) for each student. These can be purchased wherever office supplies are sold. If using page protectors, cut them so that the top, bottom and one side are open.

2. Place a Magic Cover over the textbook page to be read, so that it covers the front and back of the page. This will keep the Magic Cover solidly in place. If reviewing several pages of text, you may wish to insert several Magic Covers at the same time.

3. The Magic Covers can now be marked with transparency markers, grease pencils, or other wipe-off writing implements. Mark the Magic Covers as students are working by:
   - Highlighting the directions
   - Crossing out some of the problems
   - Changing subtraction signs to addition signs
   - Circling new vocabulary words
   - Drawing an arrow at the starting place
   - Drawing lines dividing the page into thirds

4. Ask students to mark their own Magic Covers by:
   - Doing math computation on the page, rather than recopying problems
   - Circling all the words that contain a long "e" sound
   - Underlining unknown vocabulary words
   - Marking off page sections as they are completed
   - Tracing the route on a map
   - Circling important dates
   - Writing directions or questions on the page

5. When finished, wipe the Magic Covers clean with damp tissues.

More Ideas

➲ Magic Covers can be easily used for recording assessments and general record keeping. Information from Magic Covers can be preserved, posted, or sent home by photocopying the Magic Cover over the covered material.

Highlighting Tape

Highlighting Tape is reusable, transparent, and available in neon colors. Visual learners who have difficulty with written material can use Highlighting Tape as a cue. Students who have difficulty learning in the visual modality also benefit from Highlighting Tape because it helps grab their attention and increases focus. Tactile learners benefit from extra input as they move the Highlighting Tape to different sections of their paper or textbook.

How To

1. Highlighting Tape can be purchased from several online sources.

2. Provide each student with a 5 x 8-inch index card and several lengths of Tape. Some lengths may be short for covering single words, others may be long enough to cover phrases, and still others may be quite long to cover lines of text.

With the advent of computer software programs that provide spell check and grammar correction, we have seen a decline i the emphasis on editing skills the classroom. Yet most ent writing in schools is without the use of a com- Students need to be able gross spelling errors and rstand correct punctua- other basic mechanics of writing. Good writers also need to be able to notice other facets of effective writing such

3. Have students stick the lengths of Tape to their index cards, folding a tab under on one end.

4. When the class is working with text material (e.g., a science book), direct students to take out their Highlighting Tape index card. Throughout the lesson, direct students to:
   - Highlight the directions.
   - Highlight unknown vocabulary words (come back later to look them up).
   - Highlight the sentence that answers a given question.
   - Highlight the parts of speech in a sentence.

5. Ask students to hold their books aloft so that you can scan the room and quickly find students who are having difficulty.

6. When finished, ask students to return the Highlighting Tape to their index cards for future use.

More Ideas

 ⮌ Many students benefit from using Highlighter Tape while studying at home. Consider suggesting to parents that one or more rolls be purchased for home use, or provide several strips of tape to be kept at home.

Section

Meeting Standards

Super Strategies from the author's book, *Meeting Standards: Instructional Strategies for Struggling Students* © 2003.

Featured Strategies:

- ⑤ Color Fluency Strips
- ⑥ Fortune Tellers
- ⑦ Info Ball
- ⑧ Symbol Blocks
- ⑨ Hop-Step Mats
- ⑩ Learning Links
- ⑪ Work Masks

Color Fluency Strips

Students use colored strips of acetate to temporarily highlight text material as they are reading, improving focus and fluency. The strips also provide tactile input as students move them down the page.

How To

1. Obtain several project folders or report covers made of transparent colored acetate.

2. Cut the acetate into strips that are wide enough to cover two lines of text in the chosen book. Be sure the strips include the fold from the edge of the report cover so that it can wrap around the page.

3. Ask students to choose colored strips. (Encourage students to try various colors during the first few days to determine which colors work best for them.)

4. Direct students to place the colored strips over their book pages, one half on the back of the page, one half on the front.

5. Have each student line up the colored strip with the sentence about to be read. The strip should highlight two lines of text at once.

6. As students read, direct them to move their strips down the page, continually covering the line they are reading. This will help them to keep their place, reading more fluently as they move from line to line.

More Ideas

➲ If students have individual, printed schedules, they can use colored strips to track their progress throughout the day.

Fortune Tellers

Fortune tellers are finger toys made from folded paper. They can be moved and unfolded to reveal information. Although fortune tellers have been used for years as a toy, they can also be used to teach content in almost any subject area.

How To

1. Have each student make a fortune teller by using the template in **Reproducible 6a** and following the directions in **Reproducible 6b**. Many students will have made these in the past and will be able to help those having difficulty.

2. Ask each student to review the materials to be learned and generate eight content questions and answers. In math, this might include eight squared numbers and their square roots. In literature, students might develop eight questions and answers about the story they read as a class.

3. Direct students to write their questions on the inside flaps of the fortune teller, with the corresponding answers underneath the flaps.

4. On the top of the fortune teller, students can print the numbers 1, 2, 3, and 4, write four colors (red, yellow, blue, green), four spelling words, or a four-word statement, such as "I love math facts."

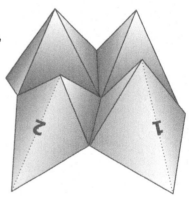

5. When all the students have completed their fortune tellers, ask them to work with a partner. Each student takes a turn manipulating the fortune teller while the partner chooses and answers a question.

More Ideas

- Fortune tellers can be fun homework assignments. Students can take them home to review material learned in school or use them to study for a test.

- Very young children may have difficulty folding the fortune tellers. For these students, you may wish to make the fortune tellers ahead of time.

- Use fortune tellers to make your reward system more unpredictable and motivating. Instead of placing questions and answers on the flaps, place the numbers 1 through 8 on the top flaps, with a different reward under each.

Fortune Teller Template

Cut out the square below to make a Fortune Teller.

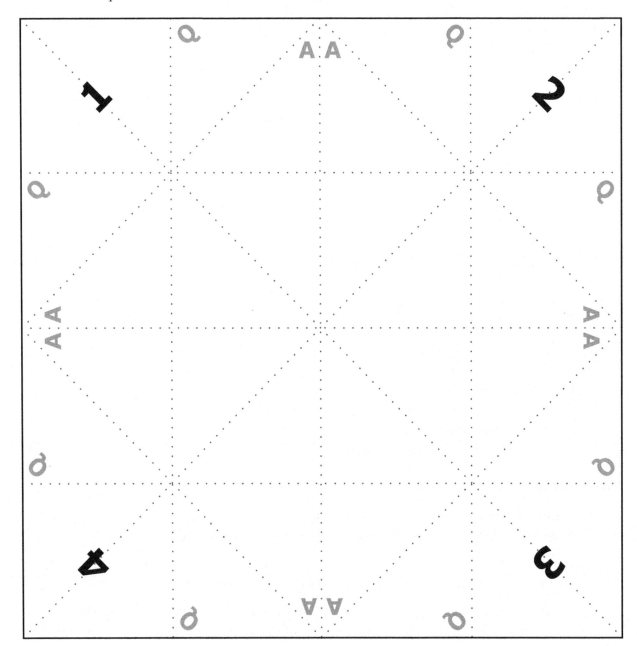

Making a Fortune Teller ▰▰▰▰▰

Follow the steps below to make a fortune teller.

Step 1: Start by photocopying **Reproducible 6a** and cutting out the square.

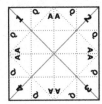

Step 2: Fold the square in half diagonally to make a triangle.

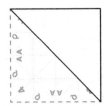

Step 3: Fold the resulting triangle in half vertically to make a smaller triangle.

Step 4: Open the paper to the original square, then flip it over so the back is facing up.

flip over

(back is facing up)

Step 5: Take each corner and fold it in to meet the center of the square.

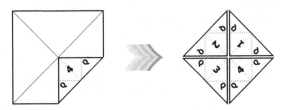

continued—

Reproducible 6b: Making a Fortune Teller, continued

Step 6: Flip the square over so that the back is facing up.

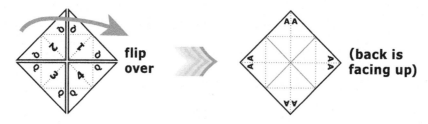

flip over

(back is facing up)

Step 7: Again, take each corner and fold it in to meet the center of the square.

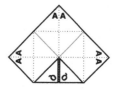

Step 8: Fold the top half of the square down to make a rectangle.

fold top half down

(top half is folded down)

Step 9: Take the folded rectangle and flip it to the right so the fold is on the bottom.

flip to the right

(fold is now on bottom)

Step 10: Put thumbs and forefingers under each flap and move fingers together toward the middle.

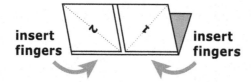

insert fingers

insert fingers

Info Ball

This multimodality, high-energy strategy engages students in practicing curriculum content. Students use their imaginations to "throw" content to each other. While practicing content in this way, students are also improving their visual and auditory attending skills.

How To

1. Ask students to stand in a circle.

2. Begin the game by announcing the topic (e.g., state facts, math facts, or science vocabulary and definitions).

3. Have one student start by making eye contact with a student across the circle.

4. Once eye contact is made, the student "throws" the information "ball" to the student across from him or her. For example, if the topic is Colorado state facts, the student might throw "The capital of Colorado is Denver." Have students use their throwing arms to simulate the throwing of a ball as they "throw" information to each other.

5. The receiver "catches" the information by simulating a physical catch, and repeating the information (e.g., "The capital of Colorado is Denver").

6. Now that student takes a turn. He or she makes eye contact with someone else in the circle and throws that person a new fact.

7. The game proceeds at rapid fire pace.

8. If a student throws incorrect information, pause the game. Tell the student the correct information, or ask for another student to help out.

More Ideas

➲ Many topics lend themselves to this game, including foreign language equivalents, story elements, parts of speech, vocabulary words and definitions, and science facts.

➲ To make the game more challenging, you can play it so that the thrower does not include the answer. For example, one student "throws" 2 + 2. Then the catcher has to answer correctly "4." If you play the game this way, be sensitive to the differing ability levels in the group, so that struggling students are not publicly embarrassed.

Symbol Blocks

Many students find abstract concepts difficult to comprehend. For these students, it is helpful to make the material as concrete as possible. This strategy encourages students to build concrete representations of their learning, thereby making it more meaningful.

How To

1. Obtain a bucket of Lego® or similar building blocks. For students in third through sixth grades, the smallest blocks are usually best. (Ask families if they have any interlocking blocks at home that could be donated.)

2. After you teach a complex concept in class, such as interdependence, ask students to form small groups.

3. Give each group a large handful of blocks (assorted sizes, colors, and shapes).

4. Direct the groups to build symbolic representations of what they learned in the lesson. Allow 3–5 minutes for students to complete their task. See *Figure 2.1* below.

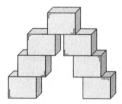

"Interdependence"

living things depend upon their nonliving environment.

Figure 2.1: Students build *interdependence* using symbol blocks.

5. When all groups are finished, ask each to explain the group's representation and how it relates to the concepts taught in the lesson.

More Ideas

⮌ Give symbol blocks to individual students, rather than to groups. Each student can build his or her own interpretation of the concept. These can then be shared in small groups.

⮌ Save what your students build and put them on display in the classroom (great for school open houses!).

⮌ Suggest that parents and students try this strategy at home. Students may build symbols that show what was taught in class or may build representations of the homework reading.

Hop-Step Mats

In this strategy, you lay content information on the floor, and students physically move through it. The content information is written on a plastic shower curtain liner with permanent marker. Once this "hop-step" mat is on the floor, students can walk on it to review content.

How To

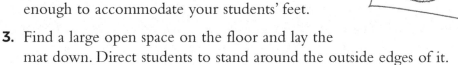

1. Obtain an inexpensive, plastic shower-curtain liner.

2. Using permanent markers, write or draw the content you want to teach on the shower curtain. For example, to practice basic addition and subtraction, make a grid of twenty boxes. In each, write a number from 1–20. For writing, draw a graphic organizer. Be sure the shapes you draw are large enough to accommodate your students' feet.

3. Find a large open space on the floor and lay the mat down. Direct students to stand around the outside edges of it.

4. Call on one student at a time. Direct the students to step on the mat and walk or hop through the content while saying it aloud. For example, call out an addition problem (2 + 7) and direct the student to hop it out, also saying the equation aloud ("2 + 7 = 9"). For a writing activity, have the student stand in the middle to talk about the main idea, then hop or step to the peripheral areas to discuss supporting ideas.

5. When finished with the mat, fold it up and store it in a location where children cannot access it unsupervised.

More Ideas

⮑ Cut shower curtains in half for smaller amounts of content (and to reduce the expense!).

⮑ Make a hop-step mat of a computer keyboard. Students can practice spelling while reinforcing technology standards.

⮑ Hop-step mats stay in place best on carpet. For added staying power, adhere small pieces of hook Velcro to the underside of each corner of the mat. If using a hop-step mat on hard surfaces, adhere small pieces of two-sided tape or non-skid shelf liner to each corner.

Learning Links

You can make cognitive connections more concrete for students with this strategy. Students physically connect two or more links, while thinking or talking about connections between ideas. In this way, students develop a solid understanding of key relationships.

How To

1. Obtain several links per student. Links can be found at the hardware store (metal chain links), from a toy store (colorful plastic ovals), or from a party supply store (plastic bracelets with an opening). Kindergarten and first grade teachers often have plastic links in their math manipulative kits.

2. As you ask a student to make connections between two or more ideas, hold one link in your hand to represent one of the ideas. When the student makes a connection to another idea, hand him or her a link to connect to yours. When the student verbally makes the connection, he or she links to your link. For example, after reading *I Love You the Purplest* by B. M. Joossee (1996), ask students to think of a special person they would like to write about. Tell them to imagine a color that represents that person. When they come up with an idea, they can tell you about it and connect a link to yours.

3. Give the connected learning links to the student to hold during the remainder of the lesson, or have the student connect to links made by other students.

4. If a writing activity follows the discussion, have students place learning links flat on a piece of paper to form a graphic organizer. They can trace the links and write key words inside the traced images as a prewriting activity.

More Ideas

⊃ If a group of students has formed a long chain of learning links, consider hanging them on display. Add a chart or poster of the ideas discussed, and you have a ready-made review of the material.

⊃ Students can make paper learning links. Simply cut 1 x 6-inch strips of paper. Have students write their ideas on the strip, loop it through a related idea, and tape the ends together.

Work Masks ■■■■■■■■

Many students have difficulty processing visual information. This is especially true when that information is embedded in a crowded field of other information (such as a storybook or text). A simple solution to this problem is the use of masks. Made from file folders, work masks can be designed in several ways to cover a portion of a student worksheet or text page. This allows students to focus on the material needed at the moment.

How To

1. Obtain enough file folders to make several work masks available for all your students.

2. Take one file folder and hold it vertically.

3. Using scissors, cut a horizontal line through the front of the folder, approximately in the middle. The folder should now have two flaps.

4. Slide the folder over the page, with one flap over the front and one flap behind the page. Only half of the page will be visible. (Now it's a work mask.)

5. To encourage predictions (and discourage students reading captions), have students place work masks over their pages so that only the picture is showing.

6. After making their predictions, students can reveal the text and read to find out if they are right.

More Ideas

⮌ Use work masks to cover worksheets so that students do not feel overwhelmed by a complete page of problems or questions.

⮌ Cut masks to fit a variety of materials. Try cutting three or four flaps, or making some with horizontal cuts.

⮌ If any students have individual daily schedules on their desks, consider placing them in work masks. As the periods pass, students slide the mask so that completed periods no longer show, and only remaining periods are visible (or vice versa).

Section

3

Engaging ALL Students Through Differentiation

Super Strategies from the author's book, *Engaging ALL Students Through Differentiation* © 2006.

Featured Strategies:

- ⑫ Challenge Questions
- ⑬ Challenge Authority Cards
- ⑭ Sticky Dot Editing
- ⑮ Personal Meter
- ⑯ Character Layers
- ⑰ Vote with Your Feet
- ⑱ Tie a Knot
- ⑲ Alternate Text Vocabulary
- ⑳ Text Retell Cards
- ㉑ Graphic Organizer Puzzles
- ㉒ Boomerang Bookmarks
- ㉓ Make a Connection
- ㉔ Group Graffiti
- ㉕ Subtraction Summary
- ㉖ Sweet Sheets
- ㉗ Participation Punch
- ㉘ Stand in Response
- ㉙ Light Bulb Moments
- ㉚ Cup Stacking
- ㉛ Pattern Towers
- ㉜ Twist and Spell
- ㉝ Spelling Keyboard
- ㉞ Colorful Speech
- ㉟ Board Relay
- ㊱ Pass the Plate
- ㊲ TP the Room
- ㊳ Stretch 'ems

Challenge Questions

All students benefit from engaging in discussion that includes higher-order thinking. It is the teacher's responsibility to ask questions and assign tasks that stimulate this kind of thinking, without getting bogged down in too much auditory input. Challenge Questions provide teachers and students with readily available questions and tasks, incorporating a tactile medium, so that all students will be interested and engaged.

Materials

○ **Reproducibles 12a–d**: Challenge Questions
○ Small bag or paper sack

How To

1. Make a single copy of the Challenge Questions (**Reproducibles 12a–d**) most related to your curriculum.

2. Cut the paper so that each question is separated and place the questions in a small paper bag.

3. At an appropriate point in the lesson, hand the bag to a student and direct him to pull out a question and read it aloud.

4. Ask students for responses.

5. Return the question to the bag for future use.

Variations

⮩ Have students generate Challenge Questions to add to the bag.

⮩ When you see a need to add some spice or challenge to your lecture, pull out a question yourself.

⮩ If students are working in small groups, such as literature circles, provide each group with a Challenge Questions bag to keep their discussions moving along at a higher level.

⮩ Instead of placing questions in a bag, tape them onto objects such as wooden craft sticks, ping-pong balls, or inside balloons. This will add an additional tactile component to the strategy.

⮩ Place each question in a separate envelope and leave the envelopes unsealed. Draw a large question mark on the outside of the envelope. Post the envelopes around the room. When in need of a higher level question, ask a student to get out of her seat, pick an envelope, and read the question inside. This gives a kinesthetic learner some opportunity for movement.

Tip

➡ Challenge Questions can be handed to students as a single sheet of paper, however, cutting them into strips and placing them in a bag adds some spice. Students are more intrigued because of the randomness of choice and the tactile interaction.

➡ For more Challenge Questions, check out **Super Strategy 41: Passing Time**.

What are some of the things you wondered about while this was happening?	Pick one vocabulary word. What short rhyme can you make up that includes the word?
How is this story different from a story you read last week?	How does this story compare to life in your house?
What would your mother think of this story?	What do you think is the most important idea in this story? Defend your choice.
If you were the main character in this story, what would you have done?	How might this story be written if it were to take place 200 years in the future?
How many ways can you think of to solve one of the problems in this story? Describe each one.	What could you change in this story that would affect the outcome?
Does this story remind you of any fairy tales or fables?	Would this story make a good movie? Why or why not?

Challenge Questions: History

What are some of the things you wondered about while you were reading?

Pick one vocabulary word. What do you think its historical origin is?

How does this time period in history differ from the last one we studied?

How does this historical experience compare to a time in your own life?

What would your mother (father, grandparent) say about this event in history?

What do you think was the most important single action during this period? Prepare to defend your choice.

If you were a leader during this time period, what would you have done?

How might this event be different if it were to take place 200 years in the future?

Pick a person who is currently famous. How would he or she have handled this problem in history?

What could you change in this story that would affect the outcome?

Does this period in time remind you of any others?

What type of movie would you make about this time in history? Describe it.

Challenge Questions: Math

What are some of the things you wondered about while doing this lesson?	If you were teaching this math concept to someone, how would you teach it in a different way?
How might your mother (father, grandparent) apply this math concept to her life?	If you were writing a fictional story that involved this math concept, what would the title of the story be?
Does this math concept remind you of any others we've studied this year?	What rhyme or rap can you develop to help someone remember this math concept?
Where might you find examples of this math concept in nature?	What could you invent that would require this math concept?
How might this math concept apply to a household appliance? Explain.	If you had to apply a color to this math concept, what would it be? Why?
How was this math concept utilized in some way in a movie you have seen or heard about?	How might people in another country view this math concept differently?

Challenge Questions: Science

Pick a person who is currently famous. How does this science concept relate to his or her life?

If you were teaching this science concept to someone, how would you teach it in a different way?

How might your mother (father, grandparent) apply this science concept to her life?

If you were writing a fictional story that involved this science concept, what would the title of the story be?

Does this science concept remind you of any others we've studied this year? How?

What rhyme or rap can you develop to help someone remember this science concept?

What prediction can you make about how this science concept will advance in 500 years?

What could you invent that would require this science concept?

How could you make money from your understanding of this science concept?

What might happen if you reversed this process?

How was this science concept used in some way in a movie you have seen or heard about?

How might geography affect this science concept?

Challenge Authority Cards

Higher-level thinking involves the ability to examine material critically and question its validity. By encouraging students to challenge authority in structured ways, we are developing strong thinkers. The Challenge Authority Cards provide this structure and encouragement and can be used on the spot with almost any curriculum.

Materials

- **Reproducible 13**: Challenge Authority Cards
- Construction paper or cardstock

How To

1. Separate the Cards (**Reproducible 13**) and back them with a piece of construction paper or cardstock to increase the durability and life of the cards (or simply laminate them.)

2. At the beginning of a lesson, choose a few students in the class who are ready to benefit from a higher-level thinking task. Hand them each a card. Explain to them that they will be multi-tasking—paying attention to the lesson while also doing the task described on the card.

3. Call on these students to respond to their task at the appropriate time during the lesson.

Variations

- Encourage students to don the role of a known authority figure as they perform their task. For example, the student might pretend to be the principal, the President, a police officer, or an authority figure from a movie. By playing a role, students may be more comfortable challenging the teacher or educational experts.

- Challenge Authority Cards can be used as part of a whole-group discussion. Put the cards inside an envelope and have a student remove one. Challenge all the students to do the task described. Enhance the activity with a discussion on the advantages and disadvantages of challenging authority, as well as the best ways to present these challenges!

- Make your own Challenge Authority Cards by writing your own content, based on the lessons you will be including. For example, in a social studies class, a Challenge Authority Card might suggest that a student look for propaganda or examples of government mishandling of an event.

Tip

- Before using this strategy, be sure that you are comfortable with students challenging your points of view. While it is healthy to foster this type of critical thinking, it will backfire if it causes you to become defensive or upset with the student.

- For more questions, check out **Super Strategy 74: Question the Text**.

Challenge Authority Cards

Listen for a point that the teacher makes that you think you could debate. Debate the teacher, using supportive examples or evidence to prove your point.

Prepare a false answer to one of the questions, and try to convince the teacher or students that you are correct.

Question the text. Did the textbook authors make any errors? Use any poor examples? Have a biased perspective? Leave out something essential?

How could you "fix" this experiment/game/situation (i.e., cheat) so that the outcome would be different?

Look for cultural bias in the lesson. Would other cultures view it in the same way? Make the same choices?

Sticky-Dot Editing

Peer editing, a process through which students provide each other with feedback on their writing, has several benefits. It provides students with practice in accepting feedback. It shows students how to think like a reader as well as a writer. And it encourages students to explore different perspectives. Sometimes, however, students are hesitant to provide critical feedback to each other or to consider suggested changes. Sticky-Dot Editing is a strategy that structures the feedback and correction process so that students can experience all the benefits.

Materials

○ Reusable adhesive dots in two colors

How To

1. Provide each student with two dots of each color.

2. Assign each color a meaning. For example:
   • Color # 1 = "Great," "Well done," or "I really liked this part."
   • Color # 2 = "Consider changing this," "Confusing," or "Could be better."

3. Direct the students to partner with another student.

4. Explain that students are to read their partner's writing assignment and place all four dots on the work. Two dots should be placed as positive feedback, and two dots as constructive feedback.

5. When each student has finished reading and Sticky-Dot Editing, have them explain to their partners their reasons for placing the dots as they did.

6. The original author of the paper then decides what changes, if any, to make, leaving the dots in place on the paper.

7. Sit with each student to conference about his or her writing. Ask the author to explain the feedback represented by the dots and discuss his rationale for making (or not making) changes.

8. Collect the reusable dots for future use.

Variations

⮑ For younger students, one dot of each color may be enough. For older students with longer pieces of writing, more dots may be appropriate.

⮑ Students can use Sticky-Dot Editing to edit their own work, too. This may be a good start for writers who are extremely shy or uncomfortable sharing their work.

Tips

➡ Place sticky dots on a plastic or laminated surface when finished. Store the dots in an envelope for easy access during the next peer editing session.

➡ Avoid using red dots. Red, in schools, is usually associated with "wrong." Students will be more comfortable providing and receiving feedback if it is viewed as helpful, rather than as strongly critical.

➡ If only white dots are available, have students use a colored marker or crayon to color in the dots.

Personal Meters

One of the goals most teachers share is to develop independent thinkers. Yet, in group settings, it can be difficult for students to feel comfortable voicing their own opinions. Peer influence is very strong. A Personal Meter is a tool for encouraging students to form independent opinions on a variety of topics.

Materials

- ○ **Reproducible 15**: Personal Meters, one for each student
- ○ Brads

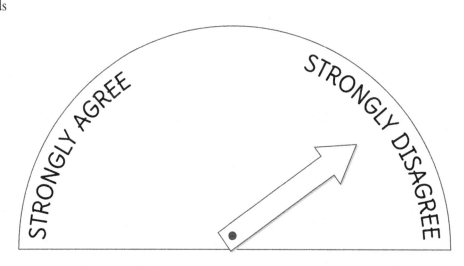

How To

1. Make copies of **Reproducible 15**, cut out the half-circle shapes and the arrows, and laminate them.

2. Attach one arrow to each meter with a brad inserted at the dot.

3. Give the students each a meter and direct them to place it on their desks, with the straight side at the bottom.

4. Choose the words you would like students to write on their Personal Meters. For example, one end might have "Strongly Agree" and the other, "Strongly Disagree." Older students might use "Pro" and "Con."

5. Pose a statement to which students should respond. For example, "Your brain is affected by what you eat."

6. Model for students how to move the arrow to point to the place on the meter that best represents their opinion on the statement.

7. Have students hold up their meters. Allow students to scan the room to see other opinions. Guide a discussion about the differences and similarities.

8. Continue with other statements as appropriate to the content.

Variations

- Personal Meters can be used to communicate a variety of things. Frustration levels can be noted by writing "I understand it!" on one end, and "I'm very frustrated!" on the other.

- Work quality can be self-assessed on the meters. Mark the meters from 1 to 10. Have students use the meters to indicate their perspective on the quality of their work.

Tips

- Place a bit of sticky tack on the back of each meter so it will stay in place on the corner of the desk.

- Be sure to use your own meter throughout the day as a model for your students. If using a frustration meter, let them see that adults get frustrated, too, and then model solutions for dealing with frustration. If using a meter to assess quality, purposefully model a piece of your own work that is of lesser quality and then show your corrections and improvements.

Personal Meters

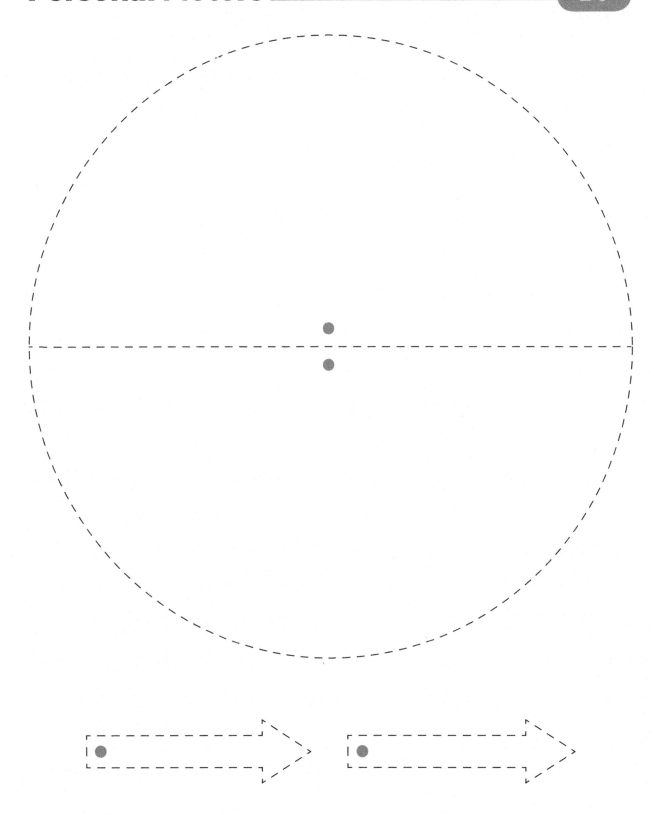

Character Layers

As students progress through the grades, they increasingly encounter characters in texts that are complex. This is true in fictional works, as well as in historical and contemporary writings. Character Layers is an instructional strategy that helps students recognize the various traits of an individual and how those traits may build upon or conflict with each other.

Materials

○ Leftover scraps of laminate or clear-plastic page protectors (available where office supplies are sold)
○ Water-based, wipe-off markers

How To

1. Cut the laminate or plastic page protectors into strips, each measuring approximately 2 x 6 inches.

2. Stack six strips directly on top of each other and staple them together at one of the narrow ends.

3. Provide each student with one set of strips and a marker.

4. Assign a character to each student. If there are several characters being studied, assign the more complicated characters to the students most ready for a challenge.

5. Direct the students to write their character's name on the first strip. On each successive strip, have them write a character trait of that individual, and draw a simple, symbolic representation of that trait. For example, if studying Brutus from Shakespeare's *Julius Caesar*, a student might write the word *disloyal* and draw a dagger. On the next strip, the student might write *confused* and draw a simple face with that expression. The words and drawings should progress from left to right and not overlap each other.

6. After students have created their character layers, select one student at a time to show his layers under a document camera.

Variations

⭕ Use the strips to show steps in a process that build upon each other. For example, the steps in photosynthesis or the layers of the earth.

⭕ Use the strips to demonstrate the correct order of the food chain, or any other hierarchy.

⭕ Make larger ones for teaching students about multiple line graphs. Students draw a different line on each layer, and then see how they overlay each other.

Tip

➡ For easy clean up, just hold the strips under running water for a few seconds and then shake them dry.

Vote with Your Feet

Ongoing assessment is a necessary part of effective instruction. Vote with Your Feet utilizes a kinesthetic response to give teachers some quick assessment information. It also provides students with a chance to share opinions and connect more personally to the content.

Materials

○ Two signs, one marked "Strongly Agree" and one marked "Strongly Disagree"

How To

1. Post the "Strongly Disagree" sign on the far left side of the front wall of the classroom and the "Strongly Agree" sign on the far right side of the front wall.

2. Instruct students on the concept of a continuum—from strongly disagree to strongly agree, with many intermediate positions.

3. At an appropriate time during the lesson, ask students to express their opinion by voting with their feet. Explain that you will read a statement to them. They are to stand along an imaginary continuum in the front of the room, based on their opinion of the statement. For example, during a science lesson that includes a hypothesis, students might vote on whether the hypothesis will be proven. Other examples include:

   • Opinion statements on political or social issues, such as, "Children watch too much television."
   • Confidence probes, such as, "I feel ready to take the quiz."
   • Content knowledge true/false statements, such as, "The square root of 25 is 5."

4. Direct the students to move quickly into position. Ask them to notice where classmates are standing.

5. Ask a few students to justify why they voted as they did.

Tip

➥ Once the Voting signs are posted, leave them up for the rest of the year. Then you can use the Vote with Your Feet strategy at any moment, without any additional preparation.

Tie a Knot

One of our culture's age-old memory tricks is to "tie a string around your finger." This quaint approach to remembering things is based on the idea that a physical act, along with a concrete product, will increase the likelihood of retention. Memory experts agree! Using multiple memory paths makes it more likely that the stored information will be accessed. The Tie a Knot strategy taps into these same benefits.

Materials

- Piece of thick cord, approximately 6 feet in length

How To

1. Hang the cord from the top of your white (or chalk) board so that it dangles down freely.

2. Choose some content for memorization that has a small, discreet list of items. For example, five steps in a process or seven days of the week.

3. After teaching the content, describe the notion of "tie a string around your finger" to aid in remembering important things. Explain to the students that they are going to use the cord and the board to remember the important points of the lesson.

4. Choose two students to come up to the board. Direct one student to tie a knot in the cord near the top and the other to write the first point to be remembered next to the knot (see illustration above).

5. Continue tying knots and writing the subsequent points until all the items are listed next to corresponding knots.

6. Have the class review the points, first out loud, then silently, and then with their eyes closed.

7. Erase the board, but leave the knots in place. Ask the students to open their eyes and silently recall the items that were next to the knots. After silent reflection, call on individual students to label each knot.

Variations

- Give each student a piece of thin cord, approximately 12 inches long. As you review the items on the board, direct students to tie their own knots on their cords.

◯ Have cords of different colors available. When trying to memorize characteristics of different items, hang different colored chords. For example, if studying the characteristics of editing and revising simultaneously, a gold chord could represent editing and a blue chord revising.

Tips

➡ Tape smaller cords onto the side of the students' desks so that they are available to them at all times.

➡ Choose the most tactile or kinesthetic students to come to the board and tie the knots.

➡ Suggest that students use this strategy at home when they are trying to memorize information for a test.

Alternate Text Vocabulary ▬▬▬

Students are motivated by texts that interest them—and, unfortunately, these are not always the ones schools have available. This activity gives students a chance to use their personal interests to reinforce the classroom texts. Alternate Text Vocabulary provides a creative structure that reinforces new vocabulary words and improves retention.

How To

1. Write the following as a list on the board or on a slide: sports magazine, teen-fashion magazine, environmental/nature magazine, art magazine, religious newspaper, sales ad, children's dictionary, comics, school announcement, cookbook, poetry collection, health handbook.

2. After teaching a new vocabulary word and its meaning, tell the students that they are to imagine that they are reading an alternate text from the list. Ask how the word might be defined and used in context in the alternate text. Provide one or more examples, such as:

   Word: *Acid*

   In cookbook: "Do not add extra tomatoes to this recipe. Tomatoes are very acidic, and the additional acid may make the recipe sour or corrosive to your guests' stomachs."

   Word: *Base*

   In sports magazine: "Remember that challenging workouts will cause you to sweat and stink. Use lots of deodorant—it includes a base that will neutralize body odor."

3. Allow students to work in pairs, choose an alternate text, and define the word in context.

4. Call on students to share their definitions. As students listen, they will hear the vocabulary used and defined several times—great for retention!

Variations

- ➲ Ask students for suggestions for other alternate texts to add to the list.

- ➲ Allow students to act out their definitions, as if they were doing a commercial, a cooking demonstration, or a reality television show.

- ➲ Instead of alternate texts, suggest that students consider alternate settings. For example, students might describe how a word might be used at the zoo, the mall, the soccer field, or a toy store.

Tip

- ➡ Assign heterogeneous partnerships so that students who need support are paired with students who are strong linguistically.

Text Retell Cards

When a student can retell what he has read, we know that his comprehension is satisfactory. When she can retell it from another person's perspective, she has had the opportunity to tap into higher-level thinking skills. Text Retell Cards encourage students to consider the text from another perspective and retell the material in that way. This strategy also provides the listeners with multiple repetitions of the content, thus increasing retention for all.

Materials

- O **Reproducible 20**: Text Retell Cards
- O Cardstock

How To

1. Make copies of **Reproducible 20**, cut them apart, and glue them to a piece of cardstock to make them more durable (or laminate them.)

2. When students are about to read as a group, pass out the cards to a few students who you feel are ready for the challenge. Quietly review the directions on the cards with them.

3. At an appropriate time during the lesson, call on one of the students to read her Text Retell Card aloud and then retell the content as directed. Give corrective feedback if necessary.

Variation

- ↻ Ask students to create Text Retell Cards for their favorite book or television character.

Tip

- ➡ Provide students with a time limit for their retelling—30 seconds is usually adequate.

Text Retell Cards

As we are reading, think about how you might teach this information to a **5-year-old child**.

Be prepared, when I call on you, to reword the most recent part of what we read.

Remember, pretend you are telling it to a **5-year-old child**.

As we are reading, think about how you might teach this information to a **95-year-old grandparent** who has never had this class.

Be prepared, when I call on you, to reward the most recent part of what we read.

Remember, pretend you are telling it to a **95-year-old grandparent** who has never had this class.

As we are reading, think about how you might teach this information if you were a **cartoon character** from television (Bart Simpson, Spider-Man, SpongeBob, etc.)

Be prepared, when I call on you, to reword the most recent part of what we read.

Remember, pretend you are a **cartoon character**.

Graphic Organizer Puzzles

Memory research indicates that graphic organizers are effective tools in helping students comprehend, organize, and retain information. This is because the content is condensed and placed in a specific location on the page, tapping into the episodic, or location-driven, memory path. Graphic Organizer Puzzles increase these benefits by adding physical movement and flexibility to the traditional graphic approach.

Materials

- O **Reproducibles 21a** and **21b**: Graphic Organizer Puzzles
- O Adhesive-backed Velcro®
- O Shallow box, such as shoe box or plastic storage container
- O File folders, one per student
- O Wipe-off markers, one per student

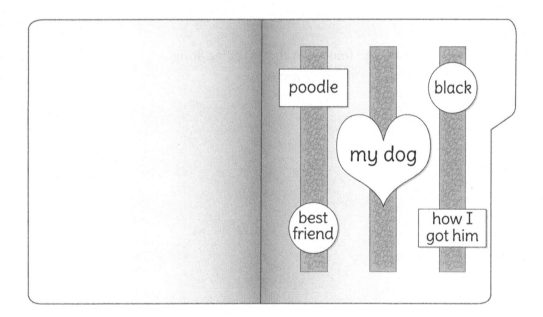

How To

1. Laminate the reproducibles and cut out the shapes.

2. Apply a small piece of the hook side of the Velcro to the back of each of the shapes, and place them in a shallow container.

3. Apply three 6-inch strips of the loop side of the Velcro to the inside of each file folder (see illustration above).

4. Distribute a file folder and marker to each student.

5. Direct the students to choose shapes they would like to use in their graphic organizers, and model which shapes might be appropriate for the assigned task. For example, when brainstorming ideas for a paragraph, it might be best to use one large shape for the main idea, and several smaller shapes for supporting details.

6. Demonstrate how to write the ideas on the shapes and stick them to the Velcro on the folder. Then show students how they can organize and rearrange their ideas as they develop them. For example, in the initial brainstorming, the supporting details might surround the main idea. But as students get ready to put the ideas into a paragraph, they can move them into a sequence they like best.

7. Direct students to store their work in the file folders until they have finished the writing or learning assignment.

Variation

⊃ Instead of using Velcro, students can apply a small piece of tape or sticky tack onto the back of the shape they will use, then stick it to the inside of the folder.

Tip

➡ Some teachers laminate the folders so they will last longer. This also allows students to write on the folders without destroying them.

Graphic Organizer Puzzles

Boomerang Bookmarks

Some students become engrossed in their reading, while others read more superficially. Boomerang Bookmarks are tools that assist students to stay engaged and attend to the content as they read. In addition, when students return to their reading at a later time, they can refer to the bookmarks to remind them of the content. Because the bookmarks are available in three different levels, teachers can match them to the student's readiness level. The author has also developed an iPad® app called *Reading Comprehension Booster* that allows students to create similar digital bookmarks.

Materials

- **Reproducible 22a** or **22b** or **22c**: Boomerang Bookmarks
- Wipe-off markers (if laminating)

How To

1. Decide whether or not to laminate the bookmarks. Laminating allows students to write with wipe-off markers and reuse the bookmarks. The bookmarks do not need to be laminated if a permanent product is desired (for a portfolio or to send home).

2. Determine the appropriate level of bookmark for each student.

3. Introduce the Boomerang Bookmarks to the students within leveled reading groups, and explain that they will be writing on their bookmarks in response to their reading.

4. Demonstrate how to use the bookmark appropriate to the level of the group and monitor the groups during the first experience. If students are successful with their use, then direct students to use them at independent reading times.

5. Have students keep their places in longer reading material with their bookmarks. When returning to their reading, they should quickly review any information they've previously written on the bookmark.

Tip

➡ To protect student self-esteem, the bookmarks are not marked with a level. The less complex bookmark has visual cues built in, and the highest level bookmark asks students to develop questions as they read. All three bookmarks allow for variation in assigned quantity.

Boomerang Bookmarks

Name_____

Directions:
Write a question for _____ of the question words below.

Who

What

When

Where

Why

How

Name_____

Directions:
Write a question for _____ of the question words below.

Who

What

When

Where

Why

How

Boomerang Bookmarks

Name_____

Directions:
Write a question for _____ of the question words below.

Who is it about?

What happened?

When did it happen?

Where is the story taking place?

Why did it happen?

How did the character feel?

Name_____

Directions:
Write a question for _____ of the question words below.

Who is it about?

What happened?

When did it happen?

Where is the story taking place?

Why did it happen?

How did the character feel?

Boomerang Bookmarks

Name_____

Directions:
Write a question for _____ of the question words below.

Who is it about?

What happened?

When did it happen?

Where is the story taking place?

Why did it happen?

How did the character feel?

Name_____

Directions:
Write a question for _____ of the question words below.

Who is it about?

What happened?

When did it happen?

Where is the story taking place?

Why did it happen?

How did the character feel?

Make a Connection

Learning becomes more meaningful when learners can connect the content to their own life experiences. This is true in all content areas and at all ages. To encourage students to make these connections and share them with the class, try Make a Connection. This simple strategy employs a tactile approach to entice students to make connections between the content and their previous experiences and knowledge.

Materials

- ○ 8 ½ x 11-inch sheet of white paper
- ○ 2 x 11-inch strip of colored paper
- ○ Stapler

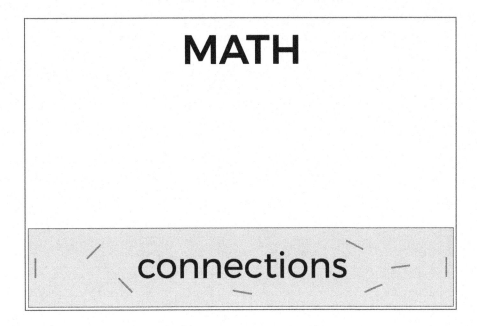

How To

1. Orient the white paper in landscape position. Across the top of it print the curriculum area, such as *Math*.

2. Print the word *Connections* on the colored strip of paper and staple it onto the sheet of paper, covering the bottom 2 inches of the sheet. Attach one staple only to each end of the colored strip (see illustration above).

3. Hang the sheet of paper low enough on a wall to be accessible to the students, and place a stapler nearby.

4. Explain to the class that when a student has a connection between the content and a personal experience, he will be allowed to come to the board and "Make a

Connection." This means that the student can attach a staple to the Connections slip and share the connection with the rest of the class.

5. As appropriate, ask questions of the student to lead the class in understanding the type of connection (text-to-self, text-to-text, etc.) and in expanding on the experience.

Variations

↪ If you would like to encourage students to develop specific types of connections, write the specific type on the colored paper slip. For example, if the goal is to help students make connections between the book they are reading and other books they have read, write *Text-to-Text Connections* on the colored paper.

↪ If you are teaching several different classes of students, set up a sheet of paper for each class. Mark the top of the paper with the class name or period. Hang all the papers in an accessible place. As you use the Make a Connection strategy with each class, the students will begin to notice how the other groups are doing. This can add a healthy serving of motivation to make more connections.

Tip

➡ Consider developing and explaining some guidelines for the quality of connections you want shared. Guidelines might suggest that students share connections that are relevant, brief, and timely.

Group Graffiti

Graffiti, or tagging, is a public form of expression with negative connotations. Usually graffiti is done illegally and with the purpose of defacing public property. But it also can be an artistic way of expressing strong opinions and ideas—summarizing them into succinct verbal and visual messages. Because linguistic and nonlinguistic summarization is a critical skill for students, graffiti makes sense for the classroom!

Materials

- 12-foot piece of butcher paper, or two 6-foot pieces
- Wide markers or crayons
- Pictures of buildings with graffiti (optional)

How To

1. Clear a large space on the floor in the classroom and place the paper on the ground.

2. With a wide marker, write the main concept being studied in the center of the paper. For example, *utopia* might be a concept in a literature unit. For younger students it might be *the world* or *citizenship*.

3. Talk with students about graffiti. If possible, show them pictures of different buildings with graffiti. Discuss the differences between meaningful graffiti and simple vandalism.

4. Have the students each bring a marker or crayon to the paper and sit down around the perimeter of the butcher paper.

5. Direct the students to draw pictures and use words or phrases to express their feelings and knowledge about the concept. For example, if *utopia* is the theme, a student might write the word *possible* with question marks all around it. Someone next to him might draw a single stick figure to indicate that each person's utopia would be different.

6. When finished with the Group Graffiti, discuss various contributions and then hang it on a wall in the classroom, in the hallway, or on the outside of the school building.

Variation

- Group Graffiti can be done in smaller groups with smaller pieces of paper. Students should still be asked to work on the floor, as it fosters a more creative, less constrained approach to the task.

Tips

- If the weather is nice, move the butcher paper outdoors, tape it to a wall or concrete surface, and work on it there.

- Help the students to understand that graffiti does not need to look neat—words and pictures can be written and drawn from different angles and even upside down.

Subtraction Summary

The ability to summarize has been identified as one of the skills that will most positively affect learning. Yet many students do not know how to summarize effectively. They may meander on and on, adding lots of insignificant detail. Or, perhaps, they miss the main idea all together. Subtraction Summary provides repeated practice with summarizing while also providing repeated review of the content being studied.

Materials

- ○ 10 playing cards, with the value of each card being between 6 and 13. (There will be multiples of some of the higher cards.)
- ○ White board for each student
- ○ Marker for each student

How To

1. Distribute a white board and marker to each student.

2. Explain to the class that you are going to read a passage from the text to them and that they are going to write a summary of what you read.

3. After the students have had time, call on one to read her summary out loud. As the student speaks, write down every word on the board (or type and project.)

4. When the student has finished, count up the total number of words, and write it in the right-hand margin at the end of the summary. For example, the first summary might have 35 words.

5. Holding the deck of cards in your hands, ask another student to remove one of the cards. Subtract the card value from the total word count of the original summary. In our example, if a student removes the 9 card, write the problem 35 − 9 = 26 on the board.

6. Explain to the students that they are to summarize again, but in exactly that number of words (26). They can use the original statement and just erase some of the unnecessary words, or they can start fresh.

7. After adequate time has passed, call on a student who has the correct number of words in a summary. Again, record every word the student reads.

8. Repeat steps 5–7 until the final summary is fewer than eight words.

9. Discuss the activity, drawing the students' attention to the fact that they were able to become more and more succinct in their summarizations.

Variations

⮑ Subtraction Summary can be used to summarize almost any learning that takes place in the classroom—a lecture, class activity, or video.

⮑ Students can do Subtraction Summary as an individual practice. In this case, each student will need his own set of cards.

⮑ If playing cards aren't available, use numbered slips of paper instead.

⮑ Students can work in heterogeneous partners to develop their summaries. This may be a helpful support for students who struggle with summarizing.

⮑ Choose a few words that will likely be in an effective summary statement. Write them somewhere that students cannot see them. Challenge students to see if they can develop a summary that includes the "secret summary words."

Tips

➡ If white boards are not available, students can do their work on notebook paper.

➡ If a student shares a "summary" that is not a strong example, use the opportunity to review and discuss what makes an effective summary.

Sweet Sheets

Book Groups, also referred to at times as literature circles, are a beneficial experience for students as they study literature. They allow students to engage in discussion about what they are reading, making it meaningful to them on a personal level. The students who might benefit the most, however, from this type of experience may also be the ones who struggle with deciding what to say during the discussions. Rather than allowing them to sit back and just listen, try using the Sweet Sheets strategy to provide some support.

Materials

○ **Reproducible 26a** and **26b**: Sweet Sheets

How To

1. Ask students to get into their book groups.

2. Place a copy of a Sweet Sheet in the center of each group, so that the students can view it from wherever they are seated.

3. Explain that there are times, for everyone, when we might need a little help to get our thinking and conversations started—and that's what the Sweet Sheet is for: to help them during their discussion if they are in need of ideas of what to say.

Variations

⊃ Consider sending a Sweet Sheet home with students. Encourage parents to use them when they are reading a book with their child.

⊃ Use Sweet Sheets during whole group discussions of books by placing it under a document camera.

⊃ A Sweet Sheet can be developed for any content discussion. For example, in science, a Sweet Sheet might include several statement starters about the scientific process, the surprises of an experiment or predictions.

Tips

➡ Be sure to make it clear that all learners occasionally have difficulty thinking of things to say. A Sweet Sheet should not be viewed by students as being only for the struggling students in the group.

➡ Pre-teach some of these discussion starters to students who might struggle with on-the-spot thinking.

➡ A Sweet Sheet is especially helpful for students who are learning English as a second language and may not yet have learned some of the necessary vocabulary for a literature circle.

Sweet Sheets

Something like
this happened to
me once…

If I were the
main character
in this story,
I would…

How would you feel
if this happened
to you?

I thought the author
was very…

What was your
favorite part
of the story?

What do you think the
author's purpose was?

Does this story
remind you of
any other stories
or movies?

"Sweet Sheet"

. . . .

FOLD

"Sweet Sheet"

Does this story
remind you of
any other stories
or movies?

What do you think the
author's purpose was?

What was your
favorite part
of the story?

I thought the author
was very…

How would you feel
if this happened
to you?

If I were the
main character
in this story,
I would…

Something like
this happened to
me once…

Would you recommend this book to anyone else? If so, whom?

I thought it was kind of crazy when…

My favorite part, so far, was…

I would rewrite this story so that…

Do you think it is a believable story so far?

I was a bit confused when…

What actor do you think would play the main character in a movie?

"Sweet Sheet"

. . . .

FOLD

"Sweet Sheet"

What actor do you think would play the main character in a movie?

I was a bit confused when…

Do you think it is a believable story so far?

My favorite part, so far, was…

I would rewrite this story so that…

Would you recommend this book to anyone else? If so, whom?

I thought it was kind of crazy when…

Participation Punch

Cooperative learning is a valuable method for enhancing student learning beyond the academic curriculum. The skills needed to interact collaboratively will be useful in all walks of life. There are many times, however, when the participation in learning groups is imbalanced. Students who are not socially adept may be passive or might be unaware of dominating the group activity. Participation Punch is a strategy that can be used to balance participation in cooperative activities in any curriculum area.

Materials

○ Single-hole punch

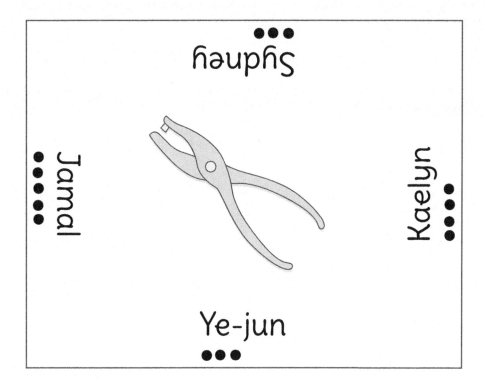

How To

1. Have students move into their groups.

2. Assign someone in each group to write the first names of the students around the edge of a piece of paper. The names should be written in order, based on where they are seated.

3. Assign another student the task of "puncher." This student will have the paper and the hole punch. Whenever a student in the group participates in any way—asks a question, makes a comment—the puncher will punch a hole next to that student's name.

4. After several minutes have passed, ask the students to pause. Direct them to observe the punched paper and silently draw conclusions about the group members' participation.

(This is done silently so that students do not publicly embarrass peers who are dominating or being passive.)

5. As the students resume their group discussions, wander the room observing. Where appropriate, stop and talk with groups about ways to increase the balance in their participation.

Variations

↪ Participation Punch can be used with whole-class activities as well. The trick is to start with the right piece (or pieces) of paper. For example, if students are seated in rows, cut strips of paper so that each row is on a separate strip, making it easy to punch a hole next to every student's name.

↪ If a hole punch is not available, try a stapler, or simply direct students to place a check mark by the name.

Tip

➡ Assign the job of "puncher" to the most tactile student in the group. It will give him wonderful tactile input!

Stand in Response

Kinesthetic interactions lead to enjoyable and effective learning for many students. Therefore, teachers need to have a handful of quick and easy kinesthetic activities that apply to a wide variety of content. Stand in Response is one of the simplest! This strategy needs no specific materials or preparation and can be used at any grade level and with any content.

How To

1. As you are teaching, ask students to "Stand up if …

   … you have a connection."

   … you know the answer."

   … you agree with another student's answer."

   … you disagree with me (the teacher.)"

   … you have ever … "

   … the word 'cat' starts with the letter 'c.'"

   … 5 x 5 = 25."

   … 'azul' means 'blue.'"

   … the capitol of Colorado is Denver."

2. Survey the room quickly and have students sit down again. Continue with the lesson.

3. Develop Stand in Response statements that are appropriate to the current content and grade level.

Variations

⮑ If there is a student in a wheelchair, try this variation: Have students turn to their right or left (standing or seated) in response to a question. The student in a wheelchair can also turn (or be turned) like his classmates.

⮑ In some countries, affirmation and approval is sometimes noted by stomping one's feet repeatedly. Explain this custom to students and direct them to use this response in class. It will give strong kinesthetic input and reinforce the response with a rousing auditory signal!

Tips

➡ Research suggests that attention and retention diminish after 20 minutes of instruction if there have been no opportunities to move. So use the Stand in Response technique at least every 20 minutes.

➡ Design statements that will get most of the students out of their seats. For example, "Stand up if you have ever seen a pyramid" is likely to get most students up, versus "Stand up if you have ever been to Egypt."

Light Bulb Moments

Videos can bring almost any content to life for students. With such a wonderful assortment of relevant material available in this medium, most teachers will use video viewing as part of their instructional program. For students who are active learners, however, sitting for prolonged periods and watching a video may result in tuning out. Light Bulb Moments gives all students an opportunity to remain engaged and thinking while watching videos.

Materials

- ○ **Reproducible 29**: Light Bulb Moments
- ○ Water-based, wipe-off markers

How To

1. Make copies of the reproducible, laminate them, and cut out the bulbs.

2. Before viewing a video, provide each student with one or more light bulbs and a marker.

3. Direct students to listen for Light Bulb Moments as they watch the video. Light Bulb Moments might include a strong personal connection to the content, something that amazes the student, or a revelation they have while watching.

4. When a student experiences a Light Bulb Moment, he is to write his thought on the laminated light bulb.

5. As students view the video, remind them once or twice to listen for Light Bulb Moments.

6. At some point during the video, write and post your own Light Bulb Moment in a spot where students will notice and be reminded. This will serve as a cue to students. When the video is finished, have students post their light bulbs on a board or wall.

7. Discuss as time permits. Ask students to share their ideas or offer connections to their peers' Light Bulb Moments.

Variation

○ More active students may benefit from posting their light bulbs as soon as they write them. If you have students who might benefit from this, be sure to choose a posting area that will not distract students from viewing the video.

Light Bulb Moments

Cup Stacking

One of the latest sports to come on the scene is Cup Stacking. Designed by a pair of physical education teachers, Cup Stacking, also referred to as Speed Stacking, is an activity requiring proficient eye/hand coordination, balance, visual/spatial intelligence, and quick thinking skills. Usually done as an individual competition, this new sport is energizing children all over the country—at recreation centers, after school clubs, and worldwide competitions! Because of its many benefits, Cup Stacking lends itself extremely well to classroom instruction.

Materials

- ❍ 20-ounce, plastic-coated cup, one for each student
- ❍ Water-based, wipe-off markers

How To

1. Have each student write a phrase on the cup. For example, if studying the food chain, each student would write one thing found in a food chain. Examples might include *grass, snake, sun, frog, eagle*.

2. Explain to the students that they are to stack their cups with others in the correct order of the food chain, as quickly as they can. The goal is to get the tallest stack of cups in correct sequence. In our example of the food chain, the cups would be stacked, from bottom to top, as: *sun, grass, frog, snake, eagle*.

3. Determine the appropriate amount of time needed, and tell the students you will say "Go" when it's time to start and will blow a whistle or make some other sound to indicate they are to stop.

4. After the first round is completed, review the cup stacks with students, making sure that the cups have been placed in the correct order.

5. Have students unstack the cups and distribute them so that each has one. The students will not necessarily have their original cup.

6. Continue with additional rounds of cup stacking, encouraging students to find other ways to get taller stacks. Perhaps a student will have a cup marked with *lion* and could add it near the top of a stack to make it taller.

7. When finished, simply rinse the cups with water and the marker will wash right off.

Variations

- ➲ Cup Stacking can be used to energize a wide variety of content—anything that has a correct sequence or hierarchy. Ideas include time lines, steps in a process, numerical or alphabetical order, periodic table of elements, periods in music or art history, musical note values, or the sequence of a story.

➲ Provide one student with a cup that has the first step in a sequence. For example, in a lesson on the food chain, the first cup would be marked *sun*. Then ask the remaining students to determine whose cup should go next. When they believe it is their turn, they should come up and place their cup on top of the most recent one.

➲ Cup stacking also can be used for categorizing and sorting. Instead of stacking in a linear sequence, students can make pyramids. For example, if sorting words that have short "e" sounds vs. long "e" sounds, one pyramid might have *egg, bed, let, gem, shed,* and *pen* stacked together and another pyramid might have *me, tree, read, eat, we,* and *key*.

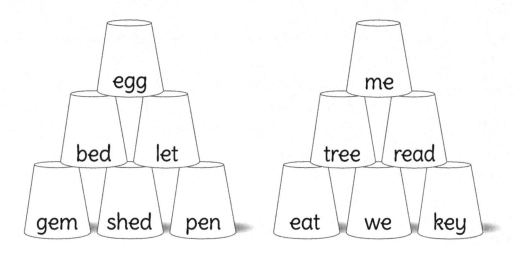

Pattern Towers

Many school concepts contain patterns. By emphasizing these patterns, teachers can assist students in grasping the concepts. Pattern Towers give students a concrete, fun way to learn things such as word families, skip counting, and rhyming words.

Materials

- Plastic building blocks, such as Duplo® or Lego®
- Water-based wipe-off marker

How To

1. Write a word or phrase on one of the blocks with the marker. For example, if teaching word families, you might write the word *cat*.

2. Show students how to connect another block to the top of the first. Then demonstrate how to add the next word. For example, write the word *bat* on the second connecting block.

3. Instruct students to write as many words as they can think of, building the tallest tower they can.

4. When finished, simply rinse off the blocks.

Variations

- Have students build towers with numbers—emphasize skip counting, prime numbers, multiples, even or odd numbers, etc.

- Plastic blocks can be used for more abstract concepts, such as elements of a community. Have students write a characteristic of an ideal community on each block, then build a community with the blocks. For example, students might write terms such as *respectful*, *diverse*, *justice*, *creative*, *peace*, etc., and show, through their block structure, how these characteristics connect or build upon each other.

Tips

- If you have wooden blocks instead of plastic, cover them with plain contact paper. Students can use water-based markers on the contact paper and then wipe it off with a damp tissue.

- Consider having students work in pairs to support each other's learning.

Twist and Spell

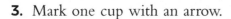

Spelling practice can be a chore for many students. Strategies that turn spelling practice into fun, while also strengthening the learning process, are a plus for any classroom. Twist and Spell, originally designed as a spelling activity, can be adapted to enhance math facts practice, too!

Materials

- ○ Styrofoam coffee cups with a wide lip
- ○ Black marker and bold, colored marker

How To

1. Using a black marker and a colored marker, write the letters of the alphabet around the rim of an upside down styrofoam cup. Mark the consonants in black and the vowels in color, and space the letters evenly around the cup (see illustration).

2. Continue to mark cups in this fashion until you have enough for Twist and Spell. One student will require six to ten cups; a small group, thirty cups.

3. Mark one cup with an arrow.

4. Choose a spelling word to demonstrate Twist and Spell to the students. For example, if the word is *child*, you will need five cups, one for each letter.

5. Stack the cups upside down and place the arrow cup, so that the arrow is pointing at the letters below.

6. Twist the arrow cup until it is pointing at the first letter in the word (for example, *c* for the word *child*).

7. Twist the second cup until the second letter of the word (*h*) lines up under the first letter. Continue twisting each successive cup until the correct letters for the word are lined up under the arrow.

Variation

↪ Twist and Spell cups can be designed to use for practicing math facts. Instead of letters, mark the numerals 0 through 9 around the cup, adding +, -, x, ÷, and = at the end. The operational signs should be in a contrasting color.

Tip

➡ To space your letters evenly, mark *a* first, then mark *m* and *n* on the opposite side. The letter *g* will go halfway between *a* and *m*, and the letter *t* will go just shy of halfway between *n* and *a*. Then fill in the remaining letters.

Spelling Keyboard

Scientists have found that language and music are closely linked in the brain, even sharing some of the same neural circuits. By combining music with semantic learning, we can increase our ability to retain information. The Spelling Keyboard Strategy does just that! It provides a way for students to associate very specific musical input with the accurate spelling of words.

Materials

- ○ Small, musical keyboard (usually under $10)
- ○ Small sticky dots or labels that will fit on the keys

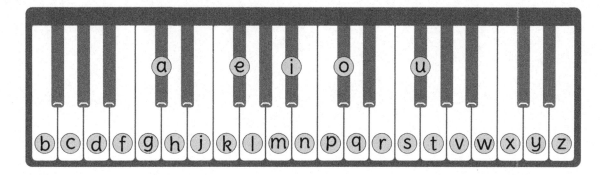

How To

1. On each sticky dot, write a letter of the alphabet, using a different color ink or different-colored dots for vowels.

2. Stick the dots on the keys in alphabetical order, placing the vowels on the black keys and the consonants on white keys (see illustration above).

3. Give a student a word to spell, and direct him to press the corresponding keys on the keyboard as he says the letters aloud. Repeat at least two more times.

4. If working with a group, ask several children to play the same word before moving on to the next word on the list. Each word will have its own unique tune so that students can sing along!

Variations

⊃ Not teaching spelling? The keyboards can be used to enhance other learning, too. Obtain three or four keyboards. Write the letters *A*, *B*, *C*, and *D* on sticky dots. Place the *A* dot on the lowest white key, the *B* dot about ⅓ of the way up the keyboard, the *C* dot ⅔ of the way up the keyboard, and the *D* dot on the highest white key. Put students into cooperative groups, each group with its own keyboard. Pose multiple-choice questions to the class, allowing several seconds for the group to confer about the answer. When you call time, students must press the corresponding key to the correct answer.

⮑ To add even greater tactile input, write the letters with colored puff paint (found at most craft stores).

Tips

➡ For center work, it is helpful to have keyboards that allow plug-in headphones.

➡ When using multiple keyboards for cooperative groups (see Variation above), be sure to place the *A*, *B*, *C*, and *D* dots on the same keys on each keyboard. That way it will be easy to hear if students are all in agreement or in disagreement.

Colorful Speech

Every school age child is taught that our language is made up of "parts of speech." There are very specific rules governing the use of various parts of speech in verbal and written communication. While many students grasp this concept quickly, others find the whole notion to be too abstract. Colorful Speech is an approach to teaching parts of speech that makes the concept more concrete and understandable.

Materials

○ Unifix® cubes, or other connecting blocks of various colors (Unifix cubes are generally used as math manipulatives and are often available in primary grades classrooms.)

How To

1. Distribute a set of colored cubes to each student.

2. Write a color key on the board, with each color corresponding to a part of speech. For example:

    Blue = noun   Yellow = preposition

    Red = verb   White = adjective

    Brown = pronoun   Orange = adverb

    Black = article

3. Explain to the students that each word in a sentence is a different part of speech, as they have been studying. Direct them to the color key on the board, pointing out that each part of speech has been assigned a color.

4. Write a sentence on the board, such as follows, and assign the appropriate color to each word, getting help from the students.

The	*cat*	*ran*	*into*	*the*	*street.*
Black	Blue	Red	Yellow	Black	Blue

5. Write a new sentence on the board and ask students to build the sentence by connecting the correct color cubes in the correct order.

6. Allow time for students to practice with additional sentences.

Variations

⮌ Using a water-based marker, write the parts of speech on the corresponding colored cubes. This will eliminate the need for students to refer to a separate key.

⮌ Simplify the activity for students by having them work on fewer parts of speech, for example nouns and verbs. Adapt the activity for students who are ready for greater complexity by adding higher concepts such as proper nouns.

⊃ If students have not yet been introduced to all of the parts of speech, design the lesson and the color key to include only those parts taught.

⊃ Use Colorful Speech cubes as a way to enhance editing skills. Direct students to review their writing and make sure that every sentence contains a blue and red cube (noun and verb.)

⊃ After students show consistent success using the Colorful Speech cubes, transition them to using crayons or colored pencils to draw boxes around the words in their sentences.

Tip

➡ If any students have difficulty with far point work, consider printing out the color key and sentences so that they can be close at hand.

Board Relay

When someone sits for 20 minutes or more, blood begins to pool in the lower half of the body. Within seconds of standing up, the blood flow to the brain is increased by 15 percent. In other words, if students have been sitting in a classroom for more than 20 minutes, the blood in the brain has decreased by 15 percent! Board Relay reverses this by getting students up and moving in a fun, fast-paced instructional experience. As an added bonus, Board Relay does not require any advance preparation or purchasing on the part of the teacher.

How To

1. Divide the class into four relay teams. Team membership should be heterogeneous.

2. Review the rules of Board Relay with the students:
   - No running.
   - No shouting out answers
   - If using dry-erase markers, caps must be replaced after each turn.
   - Marker or chalk must be placed on the ledge after each turn.
   - Winners will be determined based on accuracy as well as speed.

3. Divide the board into four sections and place chalk or a marker on the ledge beneath each section.

4. Determine the task for Board Relay. For example, students might be required to list 10 examples of the concept just taught, compose a sentence using an assigned vocabulary word, skip count by 5's to 50, etc.

5. Explain to students that they will each take a turn in completing the task, as in a relay. Depending on the assignment, clarify for students how much should be done in each turn. For example, in skip counting by 5's, each student would list the next number in the sequence. Students will most likely have multiple turns before the round is over.

6. Explain that finish times will be kept for each team, but that finishing first does not mean winning—accuracy is more important.

7. Determine and convey a scoring system. For example, finishing first is worth 100 points, second 90 points, third 80 points, and fourth 70 points. But, for every error, the team loses 15 points.

8. Start the Board Relay. As necessary, remind students of the rules.

9. Mark the finishing order of each team on the board. When the last team has completed the task, engage the whole group in reviewing the work of each team for accuracy.

10. Note total scores for each team and try again with a new task.

Variations

◯ Board Relays can be done in partners, so that no student is left on his own to complete a step of the task. Partners should be assigned by the teacher with the purpose of pairing a more able student with a student in need of support.

◯ If boards are not available, place four sheets of chart paper on the wall, one per team.

◯ Seated Relay is a variation that reduces the physical movement in the room. For Seated Relay you will need one small white board and marker per team. The student in the first position of the relay writes on the white board while seated at her desk, and then passes it back to the next student.

Tip

➡ Be thoughtful of the relay positions assigned to students. If one step of the assigned task is likely to be the most difficult, assign that relay position to a student who is more ready for the challenge. Or, if one step of the task might be less complex than others, assign a student who is currently functioning at that level to that relay position.

Pass the Plate

Developing students who are able to think "out of the box" is a goal of many teachers. Pass the Plate is a high-energy activity that encourages students to generate a wide variety of ideas, and exposes all students to creative thinking. Pass the Plate also allows students who are English language learners to be exposed to a wealth of rich vocabulary words.

Materials

- ○ Six plastic disposable plates
- ○ Water-based, wipe-off markers

How To

1. Place students in heterogeneous groups and provide each group with a plate and a marker.

2. Explain to the students that you will announce a word. One of the group members is to write the word in the center of the plate. For example, the word might be *big*.

3. Once the word has been written, tell the students that they will have 2 minutes to generate as many synonyms for the word as possible. Each student is to take a turn and write a synonym on the plate around the edge. The plate is to be passed around the group as quickly as possible. If a student cannot think of a word, her teammates can help.

4. Explain that each word will generate points, but the most points will be awarded to words that are not found on any other plate.

5. Provide common examples, such as *large* or *gigantic*, and more creative examples, such as *gargantuan* and *super-sized*.

6. After the time period is finished, help students in determining their points. Award 10 points for each word on the plate, and 50 points for any word that no other group has written.

7. When finished, simply rinse the plates off and store for another time.

Variations

- ⮑ Pass the Plate can be used to generate creative examples in a wide variety of content areas. Students can list examples of verbs, mammals, carbohydrates, science fiction titles, prime numbers, artists, etc.

⊃ Change the point value to work on more challenging multiplication. For example, each word might be worth 275 points.

Tip

➡ If there is a student who might struggle with this activity, carefully consider which position might be best for him. For example, going first or second is usually easier than fifth or sixth.

TP the Room

Children are intrigued by events with a hint of mischief behind them. When teachers capitalize on this interest, student engagement is increased. This instructional technique builds on a common neighborhood event—rolling a house with toilet paper. This usually happens secretly, in the dead of night, instead of the classroom, but can easily be turned into a more positive, explicit experience.

Materials

- ○ Rolls of toilet paper
- ○ Felt-tipped markers

How To

1. Assign students to heterogeneous groups, keeping the size at fewer than five, if possible, and provide each group with a roll of toilet paper and a felt-tipped marker.

2. Ask the students if they have ever seen someone's house that has been TP'd or rolled. Explain that they will have the chance to TP their classroom at the end of the activity.

3. Choose an area of the content in which you want students to be able to provide multiple examples of a concept. Depending on the grade level, students might be expected to provide a variety of examples of nouns, words with a short *a* sound, numbers that are multiples of 3, and so forth.

4. Tell the students that you will give them a signal to start and to stop. When the start signal occurs, they are to work together to generate as many examples as possible, writing each one on a piece of toilet paper, without detaching it from the other pieces. The goal is to come up with as many correct examples as possible, because they will be allowed to TP the classroom with as much toilet paper as they have generated.

5. Allow students sufficient time, depending on the task and your observations.

6. After you give the stop signal, engage students in sharing some examples. Then let them drape the toilet paper around the room.

Variations

- ⮒ This can also be done as a whole-class activity, with every student expected to contribute at least one example to the list.

- ⮒ Consider ways to raise the level of challenge for students who are ready. For example, if they were listing examples of verbs, these students could be encouraged to contribute irregular verbs.

Tips

- Hotels and other public establishments often dispose of toilet paper rolls once they have reached about quarter size. Check to see if you can get some rolls donated for your class.

- Give the school custodian some advance warning of this activity, so that he understands he is not expected to clean up the "mess."

Stretch 'ems

Phonemic awareness, a person's ability to recognize and manipulate individual sounds in a word, is essential to fluent reading. Many literacy programs are teaching students to "stretch out" the words as they attempt to decode or encode. Stretch 'ems make this approach even more effective by giving students a concrete, stretchy medium.

Materials

- ○ Cardstock
- ○ ⅛-inch-wide sewing elastic (found anywhere sewing supplies are sold)
- ○ Water-based, wipe-off markers

How to

1. Cut cardstock into 2 ½ x 1 ½-inch rectangles and laminate the cards.

2. Using scissors, make two small slits at the top (one of the short ends) of each card.

3. Thread the elastic through the slits, stringing 3 or more cards together. Cards should lay flat, side by side. Tie a knot in each end of the elastic.

4. Choose a word that is appropriate for your class, like *cat*, and select a 3-card Stretch 'em. Use the marker to write one or two letters on each card, forming the word *cat*.

5. Hold up the Stretch 'em and gently pull on each end of the elastic. The letter cards will separate, resulting in a stretching out of the word. The stronger the pull on the elastic, the greater the separation.

6. Draw students' attention to how the letters sound individually. Then slowly reduce the tension on the elastic, bringing the letters closer together, verbally blending them to form the word.

7. Provide each student with a Stretch 'em and a marker and allow them to experiment.

Variations

- ⟳ For more advanced students, use Stretch 'ems to work on syllabication skills. Have the student break a multi-syllabic word into separate syllables, writing one syllable on each card. The student might also work as a peer tutor, showing another student how words can be broken up into separate syllables, stretching the Stretch 'em to demonstrate.

↪ Flip up a letter and ask a student how the word will sound with the change.

↪ Use Stretch 'ems to practice math facts, leaving the answer flipped up.

↪ Use Stretch 'ems to follow a multi-step process, using one card for each step. For example, if teaching a problem-solving process, the first card might read *Describe Problem*, followed by *Determine Objective, Brainstorm Solutions*, and *Make Choices*.

Tips

➡ Make sure the slits at the top of the card are small enough to grab at the elastic. If they are too big, the cards will slide around too much.

➡ Keep a supply of Stretch 'ems at writing centers or in your book corner so that students can independently access them.

Section

4

Turning Best Practices into Daily Practices

Super Strategies from the author's book, *Turning Best Practices into Daily Practices: Simple Strategies for the Busy Teacher* © 2006.

Featured Strategies:

- 39 Focus Tools
- 40 Spelling and Vocab Shapes
- 41 Passing Time
- 42 Vegetable Head
- 43 Scrambled Eggs
- 44 Idea Suitcases
- 45 Forever Fortune Cookies
- 46 Human Machines
- 47 Mystery Box
- 48 I'm in! Discussion Chips
- 49 Bottle-Cap Sort
- 50 Lighting Up the Brain
- 51 Wow 'em Challenges
- 52 Flashlight Tag

This section illustrated by Joyce Rainville.

Focus Tools

With the advent of computer software programs that provide spell check and grammar correction, we have seen a decline in the emphasis on editing skills in the classroom. Yet most student writing in schools is done without the use of a computer. Students need to be able to spot gross spelling errors and to understand correct punctuation and other basic mechanics of writing. Good writers also need to be able to notice other facets of effective writing such as varied sentence length, interesting word choice, attention-getting starters, and the use of literary devices. The Focus Tool provides learners with a way to focus their editing and revising process on specific characteristics of effective writing. Through this focused reflection, each student will be able to make improvements that will lead to a solid piece of written work.

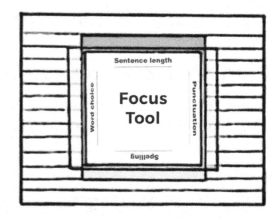

Materials

- ○ Cardstock, cut into 4 x 4-inch squares
- ○ Two sheets of acetate in each of four colors (red, blue, green, and yellow)
- ○ Tape

How To

1. Choose four characteristics of good writing that are appropriate for the level of your students. Write each characteristic along one edge of the tool, on the blank line provided.

2. Laminate the cardstock squares.

3. Cut the acetate into 1 x 4-inch strips.

4. Working with one tool at a time, tape one strip of colored acetate to the back of each edge, allowing approximately two-thirds of the strip to clear the edge. Use each of the four colors on each tool, being careful to see that the colors and corresponding characteristics are the same on all the tools you make.

5. When students have completed a draft of a writing assignment, distribute the Focus Tools. Explain to students that it is important for them to perform a focused review of their work in order to make corrections for their final copy.

6. Model for students how to slide the Focus Tool down a page of writing, one line at a time, looking through the acetate for a specific characteristic. For example, if red corresponds to spelling errors, have students look at each line through the red acetate, searching for spelling errors. Direct students to stop and mark errors that need correction.

7. After scanning their papers for one characteristic, each student should turn her tool so that another color and characteristic are at the top.

Additional Ideas

⮌ Create leveled Focus Tools using different characteristics. For example, one might have basic characteristics appropriate to the grade level, while another might have challenges for students who are ready for greater complexity (for example, these could include *alliteration, metaphor, onomatopoeia,* and *dialogue*).

⮌ The back side of the Focus Tool is blank, making it possible to use this as a focus tool in almost any subject. To adapt the tool for other parts of the curriculum, use a wet-erase marker to write a focus point along each edge. For example, in math class the four focus points might be operational signs, decimal points, commas, and answers. In a history class, the four criteria might include location, date, event, and people.

Spelling & Vocabulary Shapes

Many students struggle with accurate spelling, and spelling programs that provide students with lists of words to memorize (using semantic memory) are not always helpful. Spelling & Vocabulary Shapes is a strategy that uses graphic organizers (targeting episodic memory) to increase retention of spelling, with an additional benefit of increasing the comprehension of word meaning.

Materials

- Weekly spelling or vocabulary list
- Black line figure (see suggestions below)

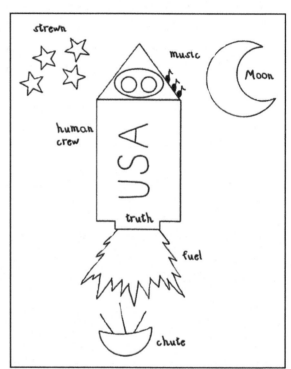

How To

1. Choose or draw a black line figure that has some associated meaning. Excellent choices include a stick person, a rocket ship, a baseball diamond, a bed, or a place setting at a dinner table.

2. Make one copy of the figure for each student, and for yourself to use as a model.

3. In class, introduce the spelling or vocabulary list for the week. Explain to students that they will write each of the words on their handouts after the class discusses the meaning of the word.

4. Hand out the student copies of the figure. Place your copy under a document camera or hang it on the board.

5. Read the first word on the list. Ask the students what it means to them. Discuss the correct meaning of the word and then ask students where it might make the most sense to write it on the figure. For example, if the figure is of a rocket ship and the word is strewn, a student might suggest that because stars are scattered or strewn across the sky, it makes sense to draw some stars and write the word strewn next to them.

6. Demonstrate where to place the word and ask students to mark their copies accordingly.

7. Continue this process for each word on the list.

8. After the class completes the shape, direct each student to store her copy in a study folder. Encourage students to study for their spelling or vocabulary test by looking over the shapes, closing their eyes, and picturing the location and spelling of each word.

9. Immediately before students take their test, remind them to close their eyes and picture the shape if they have difficulty with a word.

Additional Ideas

➲ As students get more experience with Spelling & Vocabulary Shapes, direct individuals to place the words wherever they feel they make the most sense (rather than deciding as a group).

➲ Encourage older students to develop their own shapes after looking at the list of words.

➲ Use shapes to solidify the retention of any new vocabulary. Whenever introducing multiple vocabulary terms in a content unit, choose a simple shape and have students write the terms on the shape instead of as a list. For example, in a geometry unit with words such as coordinate, congruent, slope, and symmetry, have students draw a simple outline of a car and discuss meaningful places to add the words.

Passing Time

The Passing Time strategy takes advantage of the minutes that students spend passing from your class to the next activity by providing them with a thought-provoking question just before they step out the door. The questions are generic enough so that they can be applied to almost any lesson content. Therefore, you can prepare them in advance and use them over the course of several weeks—having a built-in structure for questioning without any day-to-day preparation.

Materials

- ○ **Reproducible 41a**: Passing Time Clock
- ○ **Reproducible 41b**: Passing Time Questions
- ○ Sticky tack or tape

How To

1. Make several copies of **Reproducible 41a**. Cut the clocks apart (keeping the blank back attached to each clock face) and laminate them.

2. Make one copy of any page of **Reproducible 41b**. Cut apart the individual questions.

3. Fold the clock cutouts in half, so that the clock face is on the front of each.

4. Stick a question inside each clock, adhering it to the back circle.

5. Place the clocks around the door jamb so that they are visible as students are getting ready to leave the classroom.

6. As everyone is lining up to change classes, select a student near the front of the line to choose a clock, open it up, and read the question inside it.

7. Encourage the students to "pass the time" in the hallway thinking about the answer to the question. For example, let's say the lesson is about acute and obtuse angles, and the question is, "If this lesson were a flavor of ice cream, what would it be? Would it be chunky or creamy? Why?" Students might generate answers such as:

   - "It would be chocolate chunk, because when chocolate breaks, it sometimes has a sharp angle."
   - "It would have a tart taste, like lime, because the flavor is sharper like the points of an angle."
   - "Acute ice cream would be nonfat, and obtuse would be made with whole milk and very creamy."
   - "Obtuse ice cream would be a mix of all kinds of chunky things, because obtuse angles are big enough to include variety."

8. When students return to class, remind them of the question and ask them what answers they thought of as they passed through the hallways.

9. Change the questions every few weeks so that students will have new challenges to explore.

Additional Ideas

⮌ Encourage students to think up new questions that can be put inside the clocks. Remind them that the questions should be higher level and generic enough to fit any lessons. Show them several questions as models.

⮌ Consider other times during the week when the Passing Time strategy might be appropriate. Perhaps there are moments when students are waiting for the Pledge, finished with a test, or packing their materials to go home, when they could be occupying their brains with an interesting question.

⮌ Place students into mixed-ability groups. Choose a question and ask students to consider their answer silently. Have individuals share their answer with their group members. Call on a few students to share their answers with the whole class.

⮌ For more questions, check out **Super Strategy 12: Challenge Questions**.

REPRODUCIBLE

41α

Passing Time Questions

If you were to have a bumper sticker on your car about this concept, what would it say?

If this concept were a flavor of ice cream, what would it be? Would it be chunky or creamy? Why?

If you could go back home and change clothes to fit this lesson, what would you wear and why?

If this concept were a song, what genre of music would it be and what title would you give it?

If this concept were a store in the mall, what would it be called and what would you buy there?

If you were to find something on eBay related to this lesson, what would it be and how much would it auction for?

If you were creating a Web page for this concept, what would it look like?

If you were a ballroom dancer, how would you express this concept?

If you were to do a Google search about this lesson, what 3 keywords would you enter for your search?

If you were to develop a product related to this lesson, what would it be?

If you were to design a reality TV show based on this lesson, what would it be called and what would it be about?

If you were to put this concept into an illustration, picture, or graphic design, what would it look like?

If you were a politician, how would you campaign on this issue?

If this lesson were written up in a tabloid, what would the headline be?

continued—

If this content were to be discussed on a TV talk show, which show would it be best suited to and why?

When have you used this information outside of class?

If you were to design a video or computer game for this lesson, what would the objective be?

Given a million dollars, how would you use this information to benefit society?

If you saw a commercial on TV about this concept, what would it look like?

If this lesson were a sport, what would it be called and how would it be played?

If you were in charge and could change some part of this information, what would you change?

If this lesson were represented by a cartoon character, who would it be and why?

Where would you travel to find this lesson concept in action?

How would you text message this lesson to someone?

If this lesson were highlighted on the evening news, what would be the headline?

If this lesson were turned into a party, what would the theme and decorations be?

How could you change this concept to illustrate the opposite effect?

How would life be different if this concept didn't exist?

continued—

How might this lesson concept be related to an assembly line?

If this topic were a garden, what would you grow?

If this concept were a food, what would it be? Why?

If you were a journalist, what facts from this lesson would you include in your newspaper article?

If this concept were a mode of transportation, what type would it be and where would it take you? Why?

If this topic were a menu, what would be included?

What career would this lesson help you in and why?

If school were an amusement park, what kind of ride would this lesson be? Why?

If this concept were a pet, what would it need to grow and be healthy?

If this lesson were represented in an art gallery, what would the work of art look like?

What screen name would you choose to convey that you really love this topic?

If you had to create a CD about this lesson, what would the album and song titles be?

If this topic were a movie, how long would it be and what would it be rated?

If you were teaching this lesson to a pet, how would you teach it?

continued—

What cartoon character would benefit most from this lesson and why?

If this lesson were a vehicle, what would it be? Would it be fast or slow?

What type of weather would be most closely related to this lesson? Why?

If someone from a different country were studying this lesson, how might their perception be different?

What two or three foods would you choose to go with this lesson and why?

If you were to design a superhero to go with this lesson, what would his or her super powers be?

If you could place something from this lesson in a time capsule, what would it be and why?

What clues would you give so someone could guess what this lesson was about?

What style of shoe most represents what you just learned? Why?

If this lesson had been taught to a pioneer, how might it have changed history?

If this concept were a street, where would it begin and end? What streets would branch off from it?

If van Gogh (or another artist) had painted this lesson, what would it have looked like?

If you were to create a ring tone that best describes this lesson, what would it sound like?

Which character from a book or TV show would need to know this lesson? Why?

continued—

If this lesson had a personality, what character traits would it have? Why?

If you could teach this lesson to someone in history, who would it be and why?

If you were standing in the middle of a painting of this lesson, what sounds would you hear?

If this lesson were part of Jeopardy, what would the categories be called?

If this lesson were in a Super Wal-Mart, what department would it be in? Why?

If you developed a new country, would you bring this concept with you? Why or why not?

What season of the year would best represent this concept? Why?

Design a postcard in your mind about this lesson. What would it look like? Who would you send it to?

What famous person would be the best spokesperson for this concept? Why? What would that person say?

If you didn't know the language the teacher was speaking, what would you think this lesson was about and why?

If a famous person could teach this lesson to you, who would you choose? Why would they be good at it?

If this concept were a holiday, what would it be called and how would you celebrate it?

If you were captured by aliens, how would you use this information to help you escape?

If your favorite musician were to write a song about this lesson, what would the first line of the lyrics say?

continued—

How would you explain the importance of this lesson to the President of the United States?

If you designed a T-shirt about this lesson, when and where would you wear it?

If you were an alien from another planet, what conclusions might you draw about humans from observing this lesson?

If this lesson had a machine representing it, what purpose would the machine have? What type of fuel would it use?

If this lesson were a news article, what picture would go with it and why? What would the caption say?

If you could create a toy to describe this lesson, what would it look like? What age group would it be for? How would you market it?

What concrete model might you build to display the concepts of this lesson? What materials would you use?

Do you think your grandparents were taught this idea in school? If so, would it have been taught the same way?

You are a baker. What type of cake or pastry would you design that symbolizes this lesson?

If you were putting this lesson on your iPod, what playlist would it go under? Why?

If the principal were to walk in right now, what 5 words would you use to explain to him or her what you were learning about?

If you had "show and tell" about this lesson, what would you bring in? Why?

If you were to dream about this concept, what would you see?

What kind of an award might this lesson win? Why?

Vegetable Head

Many teachers and students find read-aloud time to be a favorite part of the day; students at almost every grade level usually welcome the opportunity to sit comfortably and listen to a compelling story. Observations of students during a read-aloud session usually yield pictures of students with their eyes on the teacher or with anticipation on their faces. But observations also yield questions about some students who don't seem to be demonstrating attentive behavior or who are clearly off-task. The Vegetable Head strategy, based on a familiar toy, motivates all students to be active listeners. It also provides tangible evidence that students are paying attention.

Materials

○ **Reproducibles 42**:Vegetable Head
○ Black marker
○ One sheet of poster board
○ Sticky tack

How To

1. Make one copy of the reproducible pages; cut the pieces apart and laminate them.

2. Use a black marker to draw a large oval in the center of the poster board, filling two-thirds of the space. Label the poster *Vegetable Head*.

3. Place sticky tack on the poster in appropriate locations for two eyes, two ears, a nose, a mouth, some hair, and (just below the head) two hands.

4. Gather your students into a group for a read-aloud session. Begin by asking them if they are familiar with the popular Mr. Potato Head toy. Point out that the head of that toy is created by adding body parts to make something silly. Explain that they will do something similar with the Vegetable Head poster.

5. Show students the laminated body parts. Explain that writers use the various senses in their writing to capture a reader's attention with detailed descriptions. When students are participating in a read-aloud time, they should be listening for specific descriptions that the author used to engage the reader. If they notice one, they can choose a related body part and attach it to the poster. For example, if the description provides a vivid visual image, then the student who notices this can choose an eye to attach to the head. If the author describes a smell, the first student to notice can choose a nose to attach to the poster.

6. Continue reviewing all of the body parts with the students. When presenting the hair styles, ask students what they think these might represent. For example, perhaps they are for descriptions that make your hair stand on end; are surprising, emotional, or confusing; or give the perfect finishing touch. Have the students decide with you how best to use these parts.

7. Begin reading. As you come across a passage that is very descriptive, add vocal emphasis so that students recognize the sense being used. Many students will be raising their hands to participate. Choose a student to identify the descriptive element and the sense associated with it. Allow the student to choose any of the related body parts and attach it to the poster. Continue reading. (If students notice multiple examples of a specific sense, you may want to discuss the example and leave the original body part for this lesson or allow students to switch out the body part.)

8. At the end of the read-aloud session, ask your students to reflect on the author's writing style by looking at the head that has been created. What senses did the author use in his writing?

Additional Ideas

➲ Create individual Vegetable Heads using file folders and smaller body parts. (Use a copier or scanner to reduce the body parts to the desired size.) Provide one to each student during read-aloud times so that everyone can individually track the descriptions being used.

➲ Encourage students to use Vegetable Head when reviewing their own writing. When a student is finished with a writing assignment, direct her to draw a head on a piece of paper and then add eyes, ears, and so on for each sense she used in her work.

Vegetable Head

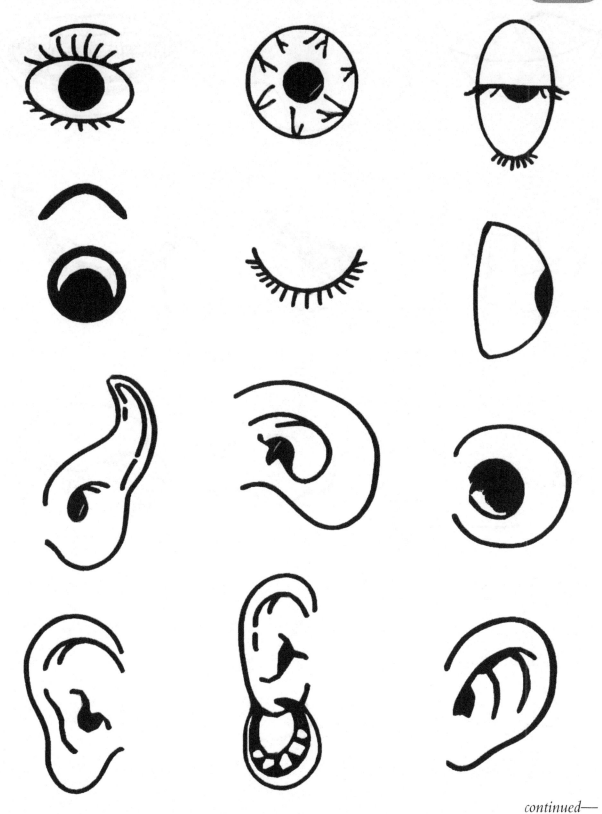

continued—

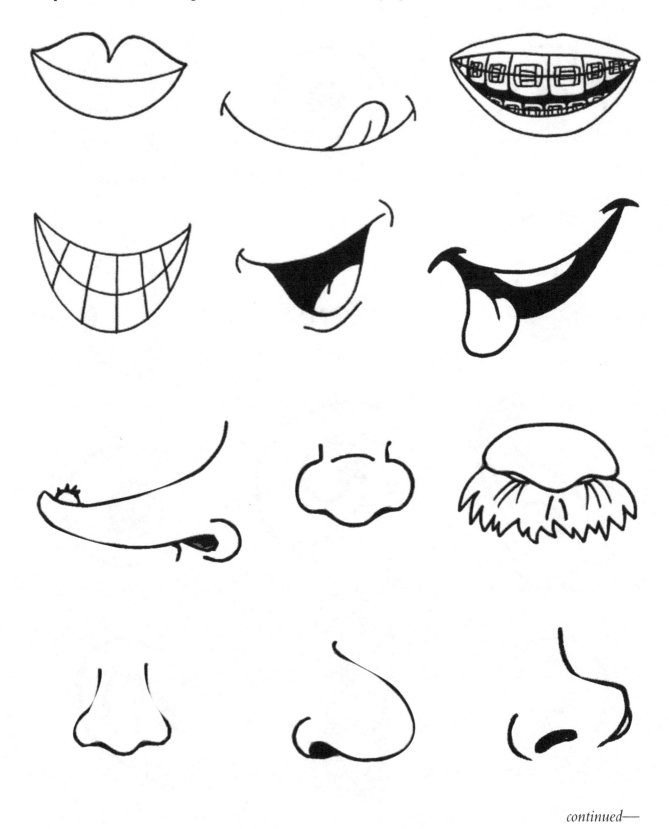

continued—

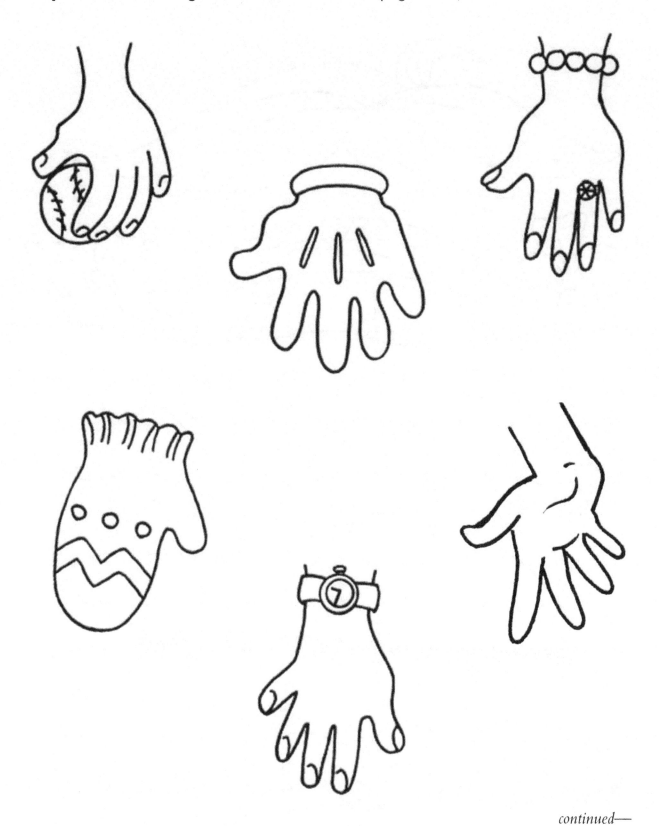

continued—

Scrambled Eggs

Creative thought and comprehension are enhanced when students are out of their seats and fully engaged in enjoyable activities. Two-part plastic eggs ("Easter eggs") are a wonderful medium for accomplishing this. Available in a variety of bright colors, plastic eggs are usually associated with surprises, fun, and a boost of adrenaline. Paired with empty egg cartons, the eggs are ideally suited for sorting by similarities or differences. Top that off with the fact that you can write on the eggs with wet-erase markers, and you have a very versatile instructional strategy!

Materials

- ❍ 50–100 two-part plastic eggs ("Easter eggs") in a variet of colors
- ❍ Wet-erase marker (also referred to as a transparency marker)
- ❍ 1/2 egg carton for every four students

How To

1. Before class, remove the top from each egg carton.

2. On the top of each egg write the name of a common object found in the home or at school. Use the ideas in the box (see next page) or generate your own.

3. Place the eggs in a bag or other large container.

4. Move the desks so that there is a large open-floor space available.

5. Divide the students into groups of four. Ask students to form one large circle on the floor, with group members seated next to each other.

6. Give each group an empty "six-pack" egg carton.

7. Explain to students that you will be pouring plastic eggs onto the floor. Show students a sample egg and explain that you've written a noun on the top of each one. Each group is to work together to find six of the Scrambled Eggs that have something in common. They should then place those eggs in their egg carton. (Remind students of the type of behavior you expect as they begin to scramble for their eggs.)

8. Pour the eggs onto the floor and step back to observe and direct.

9. When each group has filled their egg carton, call on students to explain the unifying characteristic of their eggs. For example, one group might have chosen "things that contain something" and have eggs labeled *journal*, *pan*, *book*, *pillow*, *balloon*, and *wallet*.

10. When everyone is finished, scramble the eggs again and direct students to find new similarities.

11. At the end of the lesson, ask student volunteers to rinse the writing off the eggs in the sink and pat them dry with a towel.

Additional Ideas

➲ Use concepts from your curriculum for a more focused sorting activity. For example, each egg used in a science unit might be labeled with the name of an animal.

➲ Because the eggs have tops and bottoms that separate, students can also use them to mix and match a variety of concepts. Rather than creating sets, students might pair prefixes with root words, nouns with verbs, states with capitals, numbers with their square roots, characters with traits, or words with synonyms or antonyms.

➲ Write student names on the tops of eggs and use the cartons to establish groups for a cooperative learning activity.

➲ In each egg deposit a small slip of paper that asks a question or provides a writing topic. Scramble the eggs and have each student pick one. Or hide the eggs around the classroom and have students go on an egg hunt!

➲ If plastic eggs aren't available, provide each group with a work sheet containing clip art of an egg carton. Write your words on egg-shaped pieces of colored paper, and have students glue them onto their egg cartons.

Possibilities for Egg Labels

apple	box	computer	guitar	oven	radio	stapler
artwork	brush	crayons	hammer	pan	rocks	stool
baby	calculator	desk	ice	pants	rope	table
backpack	candle	door	journal	paper	rug	tape
bag	car	dresser	lamp	pen	ruler	teddy bear
ball	cards	envelope	magnet	pencil	scissors	television
balloon	carpet	flowers	mailbox	phone	screen	tissue
bed	cat	folder	map	photo	shampoo	towel
bell	cereal	fork	marker	piano	sheets	trashcan
bike	chair	games	milk	pillow	shoes	vase
blanket	chart	globe	mirror	plants	slippers	wallet
blocks	clay	glue	money	plate	soap	water
board	clock	grass	movie	popcorn	socks	whistle
book	coat	grill	newspaper	purse	sponge	window

Idea Suitcases

Many students will be familiar with game shows in which contestants can choose to open one of several cases, doors, or curtains and uncover the prize hidden inside. Building on their familiarity with these game shows, the Idea Suitcases will generate enthusiastic interest as students wonder what each case holds. To strengthen comprehension of new vocabulary and assist in generalization, you can "fill" Idea Suitcases with labels representing "valuable vacation trips"—places students can go and use their new words.

Materials

- ○ **Reproducible 44**: Idea Suitcases
- ○ Dry- or wet-erase marker
- ○ Sticky tack or Velcro

How To

1. Make 10 copies of the reproducible. Number the suitcases from one through 20.

2. Laminate the suitcases and cut them apart.

3. Place a small dot of sticky tack or Velcro on the handle of each suitcase.

4. Using a dry- or wet-erase marker, write the name of a location inside each suitcase.

5. Fold each suitcase in half. Crease the fold well so that the cases don't pop open!

6. Hang the suitcases on a wall or bulletin board where students can access them.

7. When introducing a new vocabulary word to students, share the definition of the word and discuss the meaning. Explain to students that it is important to know how to use words in settings other than school.

8. Point out the suitcases and ask if students have seen a television show (*Deal or No Deal*) that has a similar array of briefcases, or other game shows where prizes are hidden behind a door. Explain that these cases contain the names of valuable vacation trips or places to visit. Students are to imagine traveling to each place and to think of a way they might use the new vocabulary word in that setting.

9. Select a student to come up, open the suitcase of his choice, and read aloud the trip location named inside.

10. Direct students to work in pairs. Explain that each pair is to develop a sentence that would be an appropriate use of the new word in the chosen location. Examples from a social studies unit might include:

    Allegiance, in the grocery store: "My allegiance is to Cocoa Puffer cereal."

    Regulate, on the playground: "Sara and I had to regulate the softball game before it got out of hand."

    Nation, in the kitchen: "We have foods from many nations in our cupboards."

11. Change what is written on the insides of the suitcases from time to time to infuse some unpredictability.

> ### *Possible "Vacation Destinations" for Suitcases*
>
> | | | |
> |---|---|---|
> | a movie theater | a sporting event | a restaurant |
> | a grocery store | the beach | in a car |
> | the playground | the mall | on a bus |
> | the backyard | the kitchen | a family reunion |
> | your bedroom | an art class | a farm |
> | an amusement park | a museum | your best friend's home |

Additional Ideas

⮌ Label the Idea Suitcases with the names of various occupations. Students can generate ideas for how someone with that job might use the vocabulary word in his line of work.

⮌ Write the names of cartoon characters and superheroes on the insides of the cases. Ask students to consider how these individuals might use the word.

⮌ Use Idea Suitcases to support the math curriculum, too. Place a gold star in one of the cases. Have students figure out the odds of choosing the suitcase with the star. Each time a suitcase is opened, students can calculate the odds of finding the star with the next selection.

Idea Suitcases

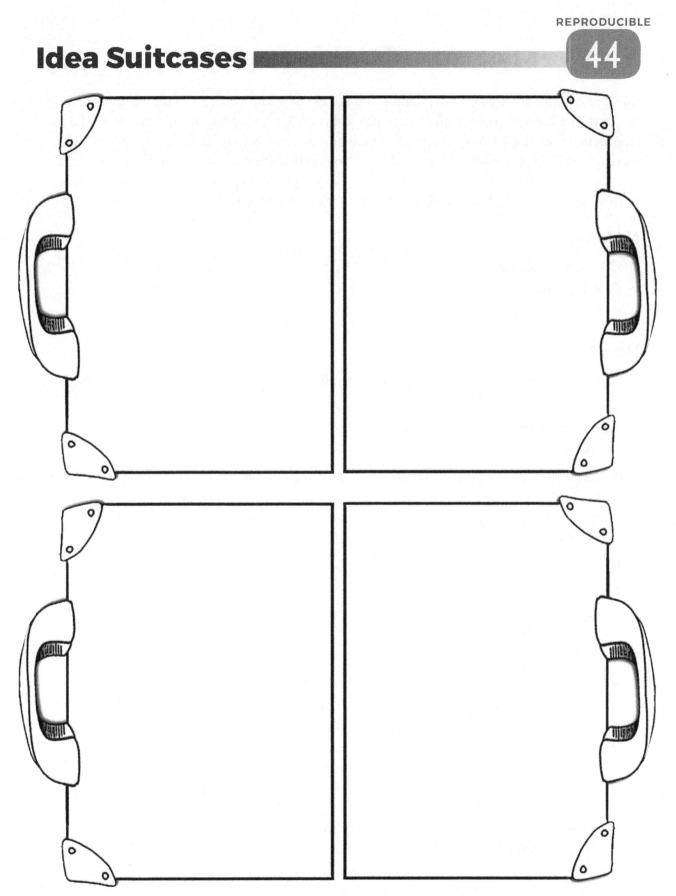

Forever Fortune Cookies

Fortune cookies are considered an entertaining way to end a meal, by combining something sweet with a forecast of what the future has to bring. Most students are familiar with the heightened anticipation associated with cracking open the cookie, pulling out the miniature piece of paper, and reading the fortune. The same anticipation is present in classrooms when you use Forever Fortune Cookies. These reusable, easy-to-make containers can hold predictions or hypotheses and will definitely hold students' attention!

Materials

- ○ Six sheets of tan craft foam
- ○ Glue gun
- ○ Slips of 1 x 4-inch paper

How To

1. Cut 4-inch-diameter circles out of the craft foam.

2. Fold a circle in half and place a dab of hot glue inside each end of the fold line. Press until dry. (In the illustration, "x" marks the spot.)

3. Bend the semicircle along the fold so that it forms an arch, with the two ends of the fold coming together in the middle. Apply a dab of hot glue and press until dry. You have completed your first fortune cookie.

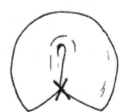

4. Repeat until you have one cookie for each student.

5. In class, generate a brief discussion about fortune cookies by asking students if they have ever eaten fortune cookies. Talk about the types of fortunes they might have found inside. Weave the words *prediction* and *hypothesis* into your discussion, helping students to clarify the differences between them.

6. Discuss and record the factors that lead to a good prediction or hypothesis. These might include the words *if* and *then*. Older students might generate words such as *related to*, *testable*, or *independent* and *dependent* variables.

7. Provide each student with a Forever Fortune Cookie and a slip of paper. Introduce the lesson and ask each student to write a prediction on his paper. For example, when starting a new novel, show the students the cover, review the title, do a picture walk, and then ask the students to predict what the story will be about. In a science unit, provide a basic overview of the experiment and ask students to develop a hypothesis.

8. Once the predictions have been completed, have students slip them into the Forever Fortune Cookies.

9. When cookies are complete have students work in pairs. Direct partners to swap cookies and read each other's predictions, discussing the differences and explaining their rationale. Then proceed with the lesson to see who had accurate predictions.

Additional Ideas

- Because Forever Fortune Cookies are made of foam, they can be used over and over again. Have students use the cookies when they predict how they will perform on a spelling test or when they estimate how many jelly beans are in a jar. Or pull out the cookies again when students guess who will win the World Series, based on sports statistics.

- Use cookies made of different colors of foam to represent different areas of the curriculum.

Human Machines

When students deeply comprehend material, they can summarize their learning in a variety of ways. The Human Machines strategy is an enactment opportunity that uses cognition, emotion, and movement to capture the main idea of the learning and burn it into memory (Wilhelm, 2002). As the learning becomes visible through the use of motion and emotion, both the performers and the observers are viscerally affected, gaining a "felt sense" of their new knowledge.

Materials

None!

How To

1. Ask students to share aloud examples of machines. Lead students in identifying common characteristics of machines. Be sure that "noise" and "moving parts" are listed as two main characteristics.

2. Explain to students that they will have the opportunity to enact emotions and themes, concepts that are usually abstract, by building a concrete Human Machine. Identify two or three main characteristics of machines—such as noise and motion—that must be present in the enactment.

3. Choose an emotion or theme that is an important main idea of the material being studied. For example, if the class is reading the classic novel *Fahrenheit 451*, by Ray Bradbury (1953), it would be appropriate to emphasize paranoia or censorship. Or, in the well-loved children's book *The Keeping Quilt*, by Patricia Polacco (1988), you could stress the passing down of traditions.

4. Pick three volunteers to build a machine. The first student will stand in front of the class and begin making a motion and a noise of some kind to represent the theme (for example, paranoia). After three to five seconds, direct the second student to link onto the first student (the machine) and add her own motion and sound. After another three to five seconds, ask the third student to join in, physically linking himself to the machine and adding his motion and sound. After a few more seconds have passed, pause the machine.

5. Ask students to react to what they observed in the human machine. Students might start by talking to partners, then offer comments to the whole group. Reflective questions might include, "How did the level of intensity match your sense of the novel?" and "What other motions or noises might depict this concept?"

Additional Ideas

⮌ Group students into trios and assign each trio a concept or emotion to depict to the class through the Human Machines strategy.

⟳ Secretly inform the Human Machine volunteers of the concept they are to depict. Ask the rest of the class to guess the concept after observing the enactment.

⟳ Use the Human Machines strategy before reading to encourage students to be on the lookout for specific emotions or abstract ideas.

⟳ Ask all students to close their eyes and visualize a machine representing an abstract idea that is part of the lesson. For example, students might imagine what a democracy machine would look and sound like. Then have students share their ideas.

Mystery Box

Mysteries quickly engage our curiosity and activate higher-level thinking skills. Many mysteries—novels, science experiments, television crime shows—are complicated and involve lots of factors. But busy teachers need simple ideas for the classroom. Mystery Boxes are simple! These boxes provide students with an unknown object and a challenge to create a connection to the lesson. Easily applied to any lesson content, Mystery Boxes result in creative, advanced applications from students who are ready for a challenge.

Materials
- One box with lid
- A variety of small, everyday items
- A journal or notebook

How To

1. Cut a hole in the top of the box lid. Make it large enough for a student's hand to fit through, but not so large that it is easy to see inside. If desired, partially cover the hole with jagged paper to make it more difficult for students to see inside.

2. Place a variety of small, everyday items inside the box. The greater the variety and randomness, the better!

3. Write or paste the following directions on the front of the box: "Without looking, pick an item from the box. Relate it to the concept we are learning. Write down your thoughts in the notebook."

4. Explain to students that throughout the week, they will have a chance to use the Mystery Box. Review the directions with the students and model the expected behavior. Reach into the box and pull something out. Relate it to a lesson concept of the day or week. For example, if the class has been studying metric conversion and you pull out a pencil stub, think aloud as you create a way to relate the pencil stub to metrics ("I could use it for a measuring stick and mark metric on one side and standard on the other" or "A pencil stub compared to a full-size pencil is like a centimeter compared to a decimeter.") Ask the students for additional ideas. If students are studying the creation of the American political system and the item pulled from the box is a rubber band, the connection might be: "The founding fathers wanted a political system with a little bit of give or stretch so that as times changed, the system could be responsive."

5. Tell students that you will leave a notebook with the Mystery Box so that they can write down in the notebook the connections they create.

6. Place the box and notebook in an accessible place. Throughout the week direct one or two students at a time to work with the Mystery Box to make connections or create relationships.

Additional Ideas

↻ Save a few minutes at the end of a lesson to use the Mystery Box with the whole class. Ask for a student volunteer to pull something out of the box. Direct each student to turn to a nearby peer and create a connection together. Encourage students to share their ideas with the whole class.

> ### *Possible Items for the Mystery Box*
>
> | | |
> |---|---|
> | pencil stub | sugar packet |
> | paperclip | piece of yarn |
> | pad of sticky notes | plastic toothpaste lid |
> | small rubber ball | rubber band |
> | miniature toys | |

↻ Ask students to bring you small items from home that they feel would be right for the Mystery Box.

I'm In! Discussion Chips

Book discussion groups, or literacy circles, are a popular approach to engaging students in active discussions about books they are reading. You may already use a variety of tools to structure these discussions while still striving for authentic discourse; here is another one you may want to add to your repertoire. The I'm In! strategy is a simple yet effective tool for increasing students' motivation to participate and simultaneously providing discussion prompts that make it easier for them to participate. You provide students with I'm In! poker chips that have graphic cues related to a variety of reading strategies they have been taught. You then encourage them to toss a poker chip into a container when they have something to say. The similarity to playing poker adds a game-like quality that enhances student participation.

Materials

- **Reproducible 48**: I'm In! Discussion Chips
- One paper plate or container per group
- Plastic poker chips (optional)

How To

1. Make one copy of the reproducible for each student. Laminate the pieces and cut them apart.

2. If desired, adhere each laminated piece to the top of a poker chip.

3. Ask students if they have ever played poker. Describe how poker players must choose to participate by calling "I'm in" and tossing poker chips into the middle of the table. Share phrases such as "get your head in the game" or "I'm really into skateboarding."

4. Distribute a set of chips to each student.

5. Discuss the reading strategy represented by each I'm In! poker chip. Remind students of how effective readers use these strategies to increase their comprehension and enjoyment of a book.

6. Explain to students that when one of them is ready to participate in the book discussion, he is to call "I'm in" and toss onto the plate a poker chip that represents the comment or question he would like to make. For example, if a student wants to piggyback on another student's insight, he should toss in the "pig" poker chip.

7. Arrange students into book discussion groups. If all students are reading the same material, then mixed-ability groups will work best. If students are reading different-leveled novels then you may want to create more homogeneous groups. Direct each group of students to sit in a circle and place the container in the center of the circle.

8. Monitor students as they engage in discussion. If you notice a student has not put in a poker chip, ask her to look at the pictures on the chips to help her think of something to add.

9. If desired, have students pause halfway through the discussion period and reflect on how "in the game" they are.

10. With a few minutes remaining in the lesson period, ask students to reflect on which chips were used and which were not. (Not every reading selection lends itself to all of the reading strategies on the chips.) Guide discussion about ways to "stay in the game."

Additional Ideas

⮌ For other lessons that lend themselves to student discussion, design symbols that represent the types of contributions you would like students to make. For example, during a science lesson, you might have symbols that represent hypothesis, procedure, observation, results, and conclusion.

⮌ Students can use plain poker chips to participate in discussions that do not lend themselves to a predetermined set of contributions.

⮌ If students have not yet been exposed to all of the I'm In! reading strategies, provide them with just a few of the most familiar chips.

I'm In! Discussion Chips

Predicting

Clarifying

Summarizing

Visualizing

Questioning

Piggybacking

Feeling

Connecting

Vocabulary

Bottle-Cap Sort

With tight classroom budgets, ideas that don't cost anything are very attractive to teachers. Fortunately, Bottle-Cap Sort is also a strategy that is attractive to students! This instructional strategy uses the plastic caps from water bottles to practice skills used in identifying similarities and differences. You can use wet-erase markers to mark the caps with words, numbers, letters, or colors and then give them to students to sort. Students can move the caps around on a table or desk top, or sort them using a Styrofoam sorting board for even greater tactile input. So ask your students to help you collect these bottle caps, and before you know it you'll have more than you need! (A quick tip: Organized events like fun runs, fairs, or soccer games are great places to collect bottle caps!)

Materials

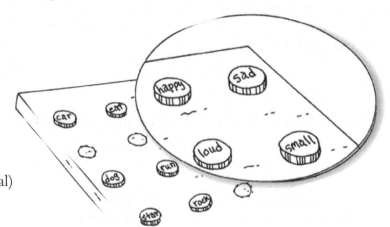

- ○ At least 130 clear plastic bottle caps from recyclable water bottles
- ○ One square of 1/2-inch-thick Styrofoam, approximately 12 x 12 inches, for every four students (optional)
- ○ Wet-erase markers

How To

1. If using the Styrofoam, score 64 circles into one of the squares by gently pushing the caps into place in an 8 x 8 pattern. (If you prefer, you can skip this step and have students sort the caps without using a board.)

2. Generate a demonstration set of bottle caps by writing a word on each cap with a wet-erase marker. For instance, the words might represent nouns, verbs, and adjectives. (In a science class, the caps might have relevant abbreviations for the Periodic Table of Elements.)

3. Using your demonstration set of bottle tops, show students how the caps can be sorted into sets based on their parts of speech. Twist the caps into different sections of the board to show the three sets.

4. Provide each student with one blank bottle cap and a marker. Direct him to write a short word that is a noun, verb, or adjective on the top of his cap. When ready, have students add these caps to the sorting board, talking about their decisions as they place the caps in sets.

5. Divide students into groups of four. Provide each group with approximately 20 blank bottle caps and a sorting board.

6. Give students directions about what to write on their bottle tops, depending on your instructional objective. For example:

   - Nonsense words for a lesson on vowel patterns
   - Nouns (or verbs, adjectives, etc.) for a lesson on parts of speech
   - Numerals for a lesson on multiples
   - Numbers for complex pattern puzzles (e.g., 2, 7, 57, 3250, ???)

7. Encourage students to work collaboratively to sort the bottle caps into sets that have similar characteristics. Suggest that they may find an outlier that will take a space by itself. Wander around the classroom and provide guidance as necessary.

8. Pull the class back together. Ask students to hold up their sorting boards and explain the reasoning behind their decisions.

Additional Ideas

○ Create temporary Venn diagram circles on your sorting board or work surface with Wikki Stix® or yarn.

○ Use sorting boards to sequence letters into alphabetical order, numbers into numerical order, or days of the week into calendar order.

○ Write letters on bottle caps and have students use them to practice spelling words.

○ Write students' initials on bottle tops. Have students talk about the ways in which classmates are similar and different (height, hair color, gender, age, number of siblings, and so on).

○ When a student makes a connection or participates in a desired way, ask her to place a cap on the board. Encourage students to make patterns or shapes as they add more caps to the board.

Lighting Up the Brain

Typically, K–W–L charts and other strategies for activating knowledge use an auditory or visual modality. But culturally responsive, inclusive classrooms need to incorporate movement as well in order to create effective learning environments for all students (Boykin, Tyler, Watkins-Lewis, and Kizzie; 2006) (Payne, 2008). Lighting Up the Brain is a strategy that actively engages students in sharing their subject knowledge and also teaches students that their brain activity increases when they make personal connections. As a result, all students are highly motivated to participate because they want to see the luminous final outcome.

Materials

- O **Reproducible 50**: Lighting Up the Brain
- O One 6-foot piece of brown butcher paper
- O A marker for each student
- O One bottle of glow-in-the-dark paint
- O One paintbrush

How To

1. Draw an outline of a brain on the butcher paper. Label the paper, *Our Class's Brain*. Set it aside.

2. Make a copy of the reproducible.

3. Show students your copy of the reproducible. Tell students that researchers study our brains to determine where we process different topics. Explain that they are unsure, but that they know our brains light up with electrical impulses when we think about things. Explain to students that you will be asking them to make connections between their prior knowledge and the new topic. If they want to, they can look at the labels on the brain map to help them generate ideas. Extend the discussion to include the fact that the brain is constantly generating electrical impulses, and that those impulses increase as thinking increases.

4. Place the butcher-paper brain on the floor and have students sit around the edges of the paper. Provide each student with a marker.

5. Announce the new topic that the class is about to study. For example, "Today we are going to begin a unit on the solar system. Start thinking about what you already know about the solar system—anything at all! If you get stuck trying to think of something, look at the brain map to help you out." Allow some quiet think time.

6. Choose a student to share something he knows about the topic. After he shares with the group, direct him to write his idea onto the "class brain." When he is finished, ask him to dab a large dot of glow-in-the-dark paint next to his statement.

7. Continue choosing students to participate at a rate that sustains attention and high engagement. You may want to have one student sharing verbally while another is still writing or painting.

8. When students have finished sharing, close any blinds and turn off the lights. Watch the excitement as the class "brain" lights up with dozens of glowing dots!

Additional Ideas

⮑ If floor space is limited, students can work on chart paper on the wall. This also works well for older students if they are less comfortable sitting on the floor.

⮑ Students can make individual "brains" by writing a variety of connections on plain paper or on crinkled, brown-paper lunch bags and painting glow-in-the-dark dots on the surface. If paint is not available, each student can place a flashlight inside her bag and turn it on to illuminate spots on the surface.

⮑ When drawing the large "brain" onto butcher paper, section off portions and label them to indicate different concepts. For example, sections might be labeled *What We Know*, *What We Want to Know*, and *What We Learned*.

⮑ Provide each student with a copy of the reproducible and have her write connections directly on the brain map. She can then store her map in a notebook and update it at the end of the unit.

Lighting Up the Brain

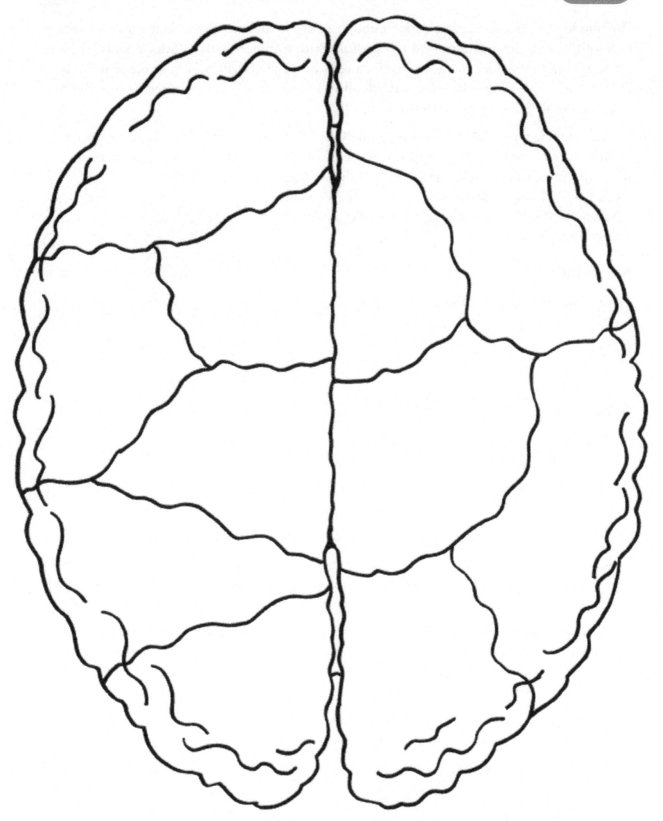

Wow 'em Challenges

Writing lessons are often open-ended enough to allow students to work at various levels. One of the recommendations of the National Writing Project is that "Educators need multiple strategies for … addressing the diverse needs of student writers." Or, as other writing experts state, "We can no longer approach all writing with one set of criteria, assuming that one size fits all (Cooper and Odell, ed., 1999)."

The same concept applies even more strongly to mathematics lessons, which often don't include a lot of built-in differentiation. Strategic lesson design that incorporates writing or mathematical challenges can ensure that students at any readiness level will continue moving forward. Wow 'em Challenges offer a simple way to have challenging tasks available on the spot.

Materials

- ○ **Reproducible 51**: Wow 'em Challenges
- ○ Two baskets or other containers
- ○ One wet-erase marker
- ○ Sticky tack

How To

1. Make six copies of the reproducible, so you have six pencils and six calculators. Cut out and laminate each piece.

2. Fold each pencil and each calculator in half at the dotted line.

3. Consider the grade-level standards for students in writing and mathematics, and then develop tasks that ramp up those expectations to a higher level.

4. Use the wet-erase marker to write one task inside each pencil and one inside each calculator. Place a small piece of sticky tack along the bottom edge; close the paper and press to hold it closed. Place the pencils in one basket and the calculators in another.

5. Show students the Wow 'em Challenge Pencils and Calculators. Tell students that these will provide them with a chance to "wow" their teachers and peers. Explain that you will occasionally prompt a student to grab a pencil or calculator from a basket and follow the challenge he finds inside.

6. When a student chooses a challenge, she works independently to complete it and then shares her work with you at an appropriate time.

Additional Ideas

○ Develop tasks at three different levels and copy reproducibles onto three different colors of paper. Coordinate task difficulty with a specific color, so that you can direct a student to choose a pencil or calculator in a color appropriate to his readiness level.

○ Generate clip art that represents your science or social studies curricula and develop it into a challenge tool similar to the pencil and calculator. For example, use a Wow 'em globe in a geography unit or a microscope in science.

○ Secondary students might be motivated by the concept of a lottery. Print the words *lottery ticket* on small slips of paper and write a variety of content-related challenges on the back sides of the slips. Place the slips in a container and have students pick lottery tickets.

Possible Writing Challenges

Add dialogue.

Add a metaphor or simile.

Use alliteration.

Use all of the five senses in your description.

Use foreshadowing.

Possible Mathematics Challenges

Develop a word problem using today's math concept.

Think of something you might invent that uses today's math concept.

If you change the order of your math process, what happens?

Look for a pattern in today's lesson.

Wow 'em Challenges

Wow 'em Challenge

C	%	=/-	÷
7	8	9	X
4	5	6	-
1	2	3	
0	.	=	+

Math Challenge

Flashlight Tag

The allure of using a flashlight in the dark is familiar to most school-age children. It is reminiscent of camping in tents, being outside after dark, or reading under the covers after bedtime. Flashlight Tag taps into these associations, enticing students right from the beginning. More important, it shifts the focus of attention to a new location in the room. By tying visual representations and discussions to a specific, unusual location—the ceiling—you help students store their learning in long-term memory.

Materials

- ○ Marker
- ○ 4 x 6-inch index cards or cardstock
- ○ Tape
- ○ One flashlight for every five students

How To

1. Using a bold marker, write a vocabulary word on each index card.

2. Tape index cards flat against the ceiling in the area over the desks. Position them randomly, with a few feet of space between them.

3. Divide students into five small groups and give a member of each group a flashlight.

4. Tell students whether this is to be a cooperative group activity in which teammates can help locate the answers, or whether they are to function independently.

5. Point out the vocabulary words on the ceiling, reading each one aloud so that students have a sense of where each word is located.

6. Explain to students that when you turn the room lights off, they can turn the flashlights on. They will hear a definition or examples read aloud. For example, if one of the words is gleaming, they may hear a definition or a list of examples such as gold, the sun, crystals, just-washed dishes, and polished silver. The students holding the flashlights should quickly scan to locate the correct word and shine their lights on it.

7. Remind students not to be too quick to follow another student's lead. Just because someone shines his light quickly doesn't mean he's shining his light correctly!

8. Students within each group take turns passing the flashlight from one group member to another. In between turns, direct the students to face the lights downward on their desk tops.

Additional Ideas

- ⟲ Write the branches of government on the cards and call out various responsibilities.

⊃ Write numbers on the index cards and call out math facts. Students can shine the flashlights on the answers.

⊃ Write states on the index cards and call out capitals or vice versa.

⊃ On butcher paper, draw the steps of a process. Call out an example linked to a specific step in the process and direct students to shine the flashlights on the correct step. For example, in a unit on photosynthesis, a teacher might call out, "sunlight and chlorophyll make sugar." The students would point their lights at the correct step in the process of photosynthesis.

⊃ Consider non-linguistic representations for Flashlight Tag. Symbols, colors, musical notes, pictures, dates, or portraits can all be used in Flashlight Tag to enhance memory.

⊃ If flashlights aren't available, post the content cards on the ceiling over open areas of the room. Direct the students to stand under the correct answer and point up.

Section

Ideas for Educators

Super Strategies from the author's website blog at IdeasForEducators.com
© 2012–2017.

Featured Strategies:

53 Progress Bars

54 Doodling Pages

55 Junk Drawer Vocabulary

56 Dig Deeper

57 Puzzles

58 Celebrity Summaries

59 The Answer Is . . .

60 Word Links

61 Boil It Down

62 Multiple Perspective Glasses

63 Participation Diamond

64 Colored Wrist Bands

65 Four Facts

66 Clock Strips

67 Frame of Reference

68 Create a Question

69 Vocab Concentration

70 State and Restate

71 Learning Journey

72 Prior Knowledge Spinners

73 Pattern Search

74 Question the Text

75 Stop for Popcorn

76 Formative Assessment Face

77 Learning Bands

78 Analogy Tower

79 Letter Bag

80 Word Toss

81 Tickets Out the Door

82 Scratch Off Review

Progress Bars

Looking for a simple way to boost students' motivation to learn? I recently read that nine research studies show that simply asking a student to write for 30 seconds about their prior knowledge of a topic resulted in them recognizing the gaps in their knowledge and increased their motivation to fill in those gaps.

Tomorrow, start your lesson by directing students to pull out some paper. Share your learning target for the day and ask students to jot down everything they know about it for 30 seconds. Then consider coming back to it at the end of the lesson and closing by asking them to add their new knowledge to the list.

A variation on this is to photocopy the following reproducible, cut at the dotted lines, and pass them out to students. At the beginning of the lesson have students write their learning target on their Progress Bar, then color in the bar based on their current confidence with the topic. Return to the Progress Bar at mid-lesson and at the end. Even if students aren't 100% truthful with their reflection, the act of reflecting will still cause them to try to select strategies that will help them meet the goal.

Progress Bars

Learning Target:

_____

0%   **50%**   **100%**

Learning Target:

_____

0%   **50%**   **100%**

Learning Target:

_____

0%   **50%**   **100%**

Learning Target:

_____

0%   **50%**   **100%**

Doodling Pages

Remember that boring meeting you had to sit through a few weeks ago? You probably remember being bored, but do you remember any of the content that was discussed?

Psychologist Jackie Andrade of the University of Plymouth has found a solution to this pesky problem. During your next boring meeting or lecture*, pull out a pen and paper and start doodling. Andrade's research shows that doodlers remember more than non-doodlers, especially when learning tedious information.

Because doodling can increase retention, consider ways that you can weave it into the next class you teach or presentation you give. Provide your learners with a doodle page connected to your content, or a thinking map onto which they can add illustrations. Below is a doodle page from a unit on growth mindset.

*If you are the one who is giving the boring lecture, then find some ideas to liven it up at www.ideasforeducators.com or www.caffeinatedlearning.com.

Doodling Pages

Junk Drawer Vocabulary

One of my New Year's Resolutions was to clean out my junk drawer. I had watched the documentary, *Minimalism*, on Netflix during my vacation and knew I needed to declutter. But as a teacher, I hate to throw things away. Instead, I decided to use my junk drawers as a teaching tool.

I gathered a wide range of items that you might find around a household or classroom. I brought it into class and told students that we were going to use it to learn our vocabulary terms. After introducing a new term and defining it, I asked students to pick something from the junk drawer collection that they could relate to the term and explain their thinking.

Here are some real student examples for the term *ecosystem*:

- A piece of string because in an ecosystem everything is tied together.

- A Rubik's® Cube because there is variety in an ecosystem and if you change one thing, it effects the other things.

- A key—balance is the key to an ecosystem

- Colored sticky dots because there are different things in an ecosystem but they all kind of stick together.

- Scissors make me think of the game Rock, Paper, Scissors which operates kind of like an ecosystem. Some have more power in some situations, but they're kind of interdependent.

Students enjoyed interacting with the hands-on materials, and I saw evidence of deep comprehension in their connections. Most importantly, I love this strategy because it is easy for any teacher to do—just empty your junk drawer!

Dig Deeper

Local stores seem to be stocking the shelves with the fun toys of summer, so I thought I would share with you a strategy for getting students to dig a little deeper.

Obtain a plastic beach bucket and a handful of plastic shovels. On the scoop of each shovel, adhere a piece of paper with one of the following higher-level thinking prompts.

- Do you see any patterns?
- Can you take a different perspective?
- Have you noticed any trends?
- Are there any ethical issues to consider?
- What relationships are obvious? Subtle?

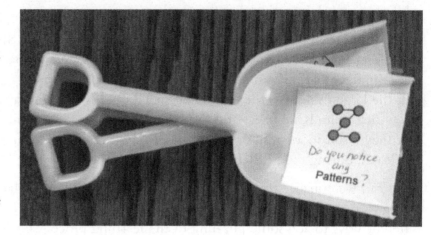

- Can you make connections across content areas?

Place the shovels in the bucket and carry it with you as you wander the room. If you find a student who is finished early, or just needs some higher-level stimulation, ask them to take a shovel from the bucket and dig deeper into the content.

Puzzles

Can Puzzle Obsession Increase Your Learning?

I have just finished playing another hand of Solitaire, my fifth in a row. Before that it was several games of Red Herring and Cut the Rope. While I enjoy the win, it is more about the process for me—the puzzling, persevering, trying to figure it out. So, rather than quitting while I>m ahead, I continue on for another round.

Neuroscientists (Panksepp, et. al) explain this experience as the SEEKING System. As our brains engage in productive struggle, dopamine is released. Dopamine is one of the neurotransmitters that make us feel pleasure and a desire to persevere. Scientists used to believe that the largest release of dopamine occurred upon successful task completion. They now know that opioids are released upon completion instead. Opioids differ from dopamine in that they result in a boost, or high, that drops off quickly. Dopamine, a more long-lasting high, is released during the SEEKING, or puzzling, process.

How can we enhance this process during prescribed lessons? Many teachers struggle with trying to make scripted lessons more engaging for all students. In a recent unit, I tried three different ways to add some puzzling to the learning process. Each of these ideas could be developed for any content or grade level, with very little teacher prep. Students were attentive and highly motivated to complete the puzzles.

1. Crossword Puzzles—I used a free online puzzle maker to create a simple crossword puzzle with the key vocabulary words.

2. Fill in the Blank—I turned the learning target into a fill in the blank puzzle.

3. Wheel of Fortune—A variation on the television show *Wheel of Fortune*. I provided some of the letters and then had teams compete to fill in the rest.

Celebrity Summaries

A principle called the "primacy-recency effect" refers to the fact that most people remember best what they hear first and last within a lesson. This is one of the reasons that it is so important for teachers to purposefully plan an activator and closure component in each lesson.

One of my favorite closure activities is called Celebrity Summaries. I made up cards that look like the ones on the following reproducible, with a variety of celebrities. Make sure you choose celebrities your students will know. After placing students in small groups, I have them choose a card and develop a brief summary or review of the lesson from that celebrity's perspective.

Some of the celebrities your students might know include:

- ⟳ Superman
- ⟳ Wicked Witch of the West
- ⟳ The President of the United States
- ⟳ Dr. Seuss
- ⟳ Alex Trebek
- ⟳ Sponge Bob
- ⟳ Katy Perry

I had the opportunity to model this activity with teachers attending a workshop I gave on inclusion. Here's one that a group wrote using Dr. Seuss as their celebrity:

We learned inclusion, yes we did
Taking data, graphs and grids.
Get kids moving on their feet
So they don't miss a single beat.
The kids are "ours," not "yours" or "mine"
15% smarter off their behinds.
With games, techniques and apps galore
This class was surely not a bore!

Celebrity Summaries

You are invited ...

*... to summarize
this information
as if you were*

Dr. Seuss

You are invited ...

*... to summarize
this information
as if you were*

_____

You are invited ...

*... to summarize
this information
as if you were*

_____

You are invited ...

*... to summarize
this information
as if you were*

_____

The Answer Is . . .

The answer is … a square. What is the question?

Many of you might think something like, "What is a four-sided shape with four right angles?" If so, you are correct! But you would also be correct if you thought:

- ➲ "What was an old-fashioned, boring person called in the 1960s?"

- ➲ "What shape is used in the game of hop-scotch?"

- ➲ "What shape are Wheat Thins?"

- ➲ "What word rhymes with *rare* but starts with *sq*?"

Now consider this one.

The answer is … jumping. What is the question?

- ➲ "What do you call a Mexican bean that moves?"

- ➲ "What is the boy doing on the trampoline?"

- ➲ "What was she doing when she won the award?"

- ➲ "How does a frog move from lily pad to lily pad?"

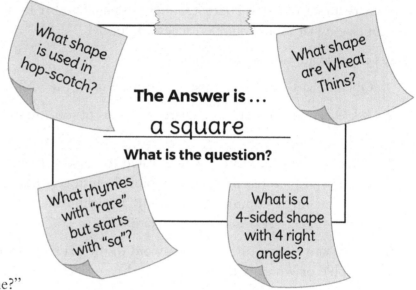

Creative thinking comes naturally to some of us, but for others it takes practice. The Answer Is … Strategy is easy to integrate into any class to get your students to think "out of the square box." Simply laminate a small poster and leave sticky notes or dry erase markers nearby. Students can share their answers whenever they have a free moment.

Word Links

When I was a child, my father and I would play Scrabble® on Sunday afternoons. It was a quiet time for us to share our love of words and be engaged with each other. In my mind, I was really great at the game—often beating my father. Now that I am a parent myself, I realize that he probably let me win occasionally.

My daughter's generation is more inclined to play Words with Friends® on their devices, but I still prefer the immediacy and face-to-face engagement of Scrabble. Whatever your preference, these word games are an effective way to activate our learners' prior knowledge and vocabulary about our class content. Simple to play, familiar to most, and easy to integrate into any course—what more could a teacher ask for?

Here's my favorite way of doing it:

1. Obtain chart-sized graph paper and hang it on the walls around your room.

2. Ask everyone to stand by a chart in groups of four, and then divide into two teams of two.

3. Direct students to write a word, related to your content, in the middle of the chart. For example, if I am teaching about Colorado history, I might assign the word *expansion*. If I am teaching a communications unit, I might assign the word *listening*. Long words make it easier for students to get started.

4. Each team takes a turn adding a word to the grid, following rules similar to those of Scrabble or Words with Friends, i.e. adjacent letters have to form a new word.

5. Let the game progress for a few minutes and then discuss with the large group some of the common words and unusual words you see on the charts.

On the following page is a reproducible that your students can use for playing Word Links at their desks.

Word Links

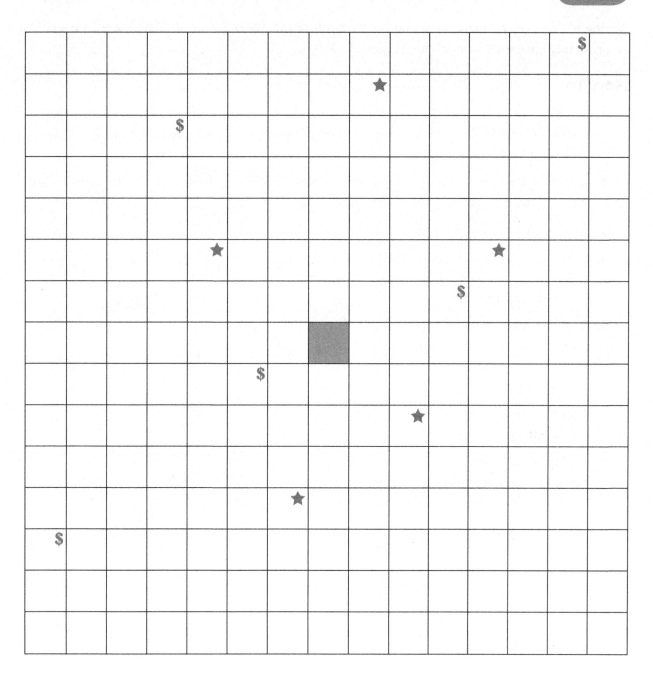

Scoring

➡ 1 point for each letter

➡ Double points for any word landing on a star (★)

➡ Triple points for any word landing on a dollar sign ($)

Boil It Down

Analogies can boost engagement and understanding for many common tasks. One of my favorite analogies for summarizing is Boil It Down.

How To

1. Ask students if they have ever watched a parent or friend boil down a sauce or gravy on the stove. Discuss how the sauce simmers, steam rises, reducing the liquid, and the sauce becomes thicker, more intense—leaving the essence of flavor.

2. Once students make this connection, compare "boiling it down" to summarizing—how we get rid of the excess and retain the essence.

3. Post or draw a saucepan picture on the board.

4. Ask a student to summarize the lesson (or book, video, etc.) and write their entire statement on the board in the pot.

5. Then provide each student with paper circles and ask them to write a word on the circle that is not necessary—that could evaporate.

6. Post the circles above the pan, crossing them out in the pan.

7. Continue until the words left in the pan represent the most important parts or the essence of the lesson. This becomes your summary statement.

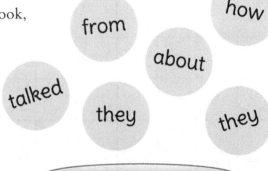

Multiple Perspective Glasses

A simple way to add rigor and deep comprehension to any lesson is to ask students to consider a different perspective. To make this more concrete and engaging, try the Multiple Perspective Glasses strategy.

How To

1. Purchase inexpensive plastic sunglasses from a party store or toy store near you.

2. Use a water-based wipe-off marker to write names on the lenses of the glasses. For example, if your lesson is on the Revolutionary War, you might write *Paul Revere*, *The Redcoats*, *Benedict Arnold*, etc. To increase the rigor, consider adding non-human perspectives, such as *The Horses*, *The Ground*, *Boston Harbor*.

3. Place the glasses in a box or basket.

4. Put students in small groups or pairs. Ask them to each grab a pair of glasses.

5. Direct students to consider the topic or question from that particular perspective. For example, "How did your person or thing feel about the American Revolution at this point in time?" The student group with *The Ground* might respond "I am tired of being blood soaked and trodden upon."

6. Have students share their thinking.

Participation Diamond

I had the good fortune to visit a co-taught classroom in Menasha, WI where I saw this on student desks.

Each student in the group of four was expected to participate in discussion about a text, offering two predictions and sharing an idea at least once. The teachers, rather than just telling this direction, created a reminder for the students, and a place for them to initial when they had completed the assignment. This provided the prompting some students needed, and the accountability that others needed.

I loved how well this worked, but wanted it to be easily reusable. I played around on my computer to line things up, and came up with this generic form, which I then laminated.

The teacher can direct students to write on the lines with a dry erase marker, then initial in the boxes. For example, the teacher may want students to offer two ideas and one question, use the word "variable" twice in the discussion and the word "equivalent" once, or use two different talking stems. This diamond can also be used for raising your hand, offering help, praising a peer—all kinds of behavioral goals. It's so flexible!

Participation Diamond

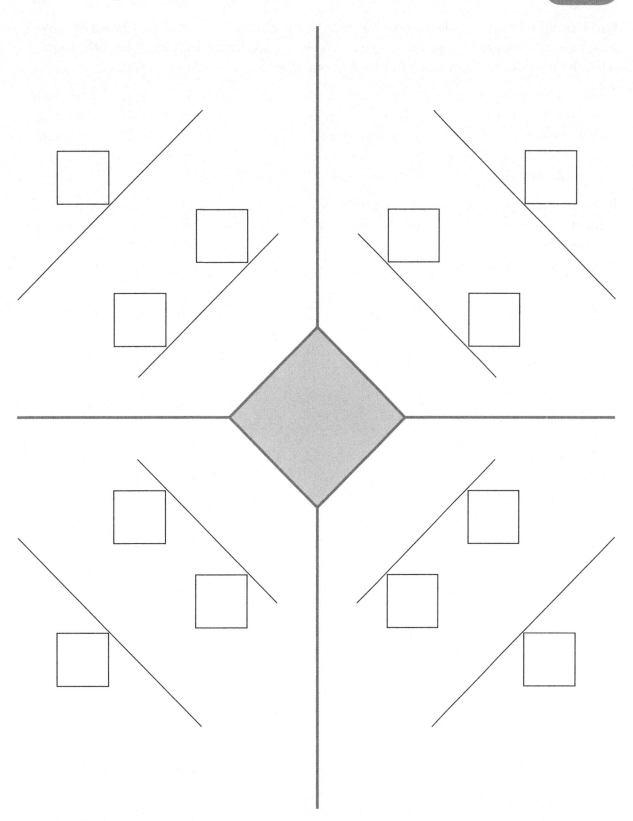

Colored Wrist Bands

Small group work is a staple in most classrooms, especially co-taught classes. Small groups might be differentiated by readiness level, activity or cooperative learning roles. No matter what the purpose, teachers want an easy, smooth way to have students transition.

I tried a new approach to small group organization and transition and it worked really well! I purchased a rubber band ball at the office supply store and then pulled off red, yellow, green and blue bands. We handed each student a rubber band, intentionally choosing who would receive each color. (The activity was color-coded by difficulty level, known only to the teachers.) Students were directed to wear the rubber band on their wrists.

It was so simple to then group and regroup by color band, to call on students with a specific color, ask students to go to a colored poster, etc. Students could easily remember their assignments—no more "Where am I supposed to be?" or "What am I supposed to do?"

You can also use ponytail holders or purchase promotional wrist bands online.

Four Facts

Boost Informative Writing with the Four Facts Strategy

Glancing through student journals at their daily writing entries, you will probably see that most entries are fiction or personal narrative. Perhaps students are most comfortable with these styles, or don't have enough time to do extensive research on a topic. Yet, we want students to gain more experience with informative writing than the occasional unit or assignment provides. To encourage students to write informational text more often, try the Four Facts strategy.

Explain to students that informational text always includes accurate information or facts. When choosing a topic, it is essential that the student picks a topic that they know at least four facts about. Just because a topic sounds interesting ("robotics!") doesn't mean they will know enough facts to do a quick write.

Provide students with four colored sticky dots. Direct them to reflect silently, listing and counting the facts they know about their chosen topic. Once they are sure they know the topic well, direct them to capture each fact by writing a word or phrase on a sticky dot.

Next, ask students to partner with a peer. Student A shares his four facts, while Student B listens and evaluates—"Is it a fact or opinion?" Some students like to stick the dots on their fingertips and hold them up to show their partner. The dots serve as a tactile, concrete way to emphasize the importance of facts for informative writing.

If Student B believes that one idea is not really a fact, encourage both students to expand on their thinking, justifying their opinions, and then ask partners to swap roles.

When students begin writing, their dots serve as reminders and can be placed in the journal to show where they have been incorporated.

After this initial lesson, keep dots readily accessible in the classroom so that students may be motivated to write informative text more often.

Clock Strips

Many students struggle with planning how to spend their independent work time. To teach them this important skill, students were given Clock Strips with three clocks, labeled start time, halfway and finish time. At the beginning of a work activity, students were directed to look at the clock and jot down the start time. Students were then told how long they had (i.e. 20 minutes) and directed to calculate and note the finish time. Finally, they were asked to determine the midpoint and mark it on the halfway clock.

As students were working, we noticed many of them checking the clock and telling their group members how much time was left. Their awareness of time, and the need to be more productive and efficient, had clearly improved! Continue the Clock Strips strategy for several weeks, and then fade it so that students are writing the time directly on their papers or notebooks.

Clock Strips

Start Time

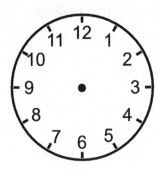

_____

Start Time

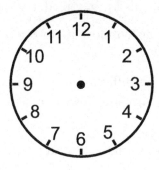

_____

Start Time

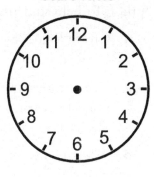

_____

Halfway

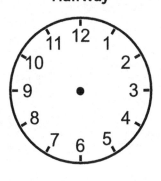

_____

Halfway

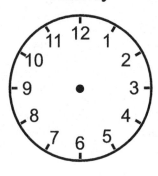

_____

Halfway

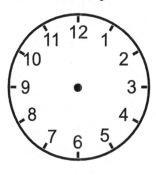

_____

Finish Time

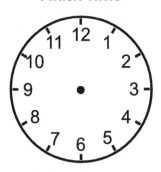

_____

Finish Time

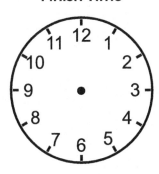

_____

Finish Time

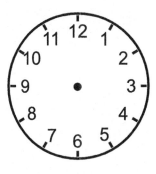

_____

Frame of Reference

Text often contains a subtle (or not so subtle!) bias brought to the subject matter by the author. To help students be aware of this as they read, try the Frame of Reference strategy.

1. Create frames by cutting a large window in an 8 ½ by 11-inch piece of cardstock. Laminate these.

2. Show students two paintings by different artists, and discuss how the artists' lives impacted their perspectives. Compare this to an artist's signature—the unique stamp that claims a work of art.

3. Ask students this question: How might a writer's life experiences influence his/her writing?

4. Provide students with a frame and a piece of writing. Ask them to find out as much as they can about the author and write their findings around the edges of the frame. Suggest that this is like the author's signature or stamp on the work.

5. Have students discuss how the author's experience might have influenced the text.

   • How has your perspective on this writing changed with knowledge of the author?

   • Do you see any examples of bias?

   • How does author information affect a reader?

   • How do your life experiences influence your writing?

   • Do you write with bias?

---

moved to Knoxville, TN at age 16

Frances Hodgson Burnett

she had always been taken care of, she supposed she always would she would like to know if she was going to nice people, who wou her her own way as her Ayah and the other native servants had do

She knew that she was not going to stay at the English clergyman at first. She did not want to stay. The English clergyman was poor all the same age and they wore shabby clothes and were always qu from each other. Mary hated their untidy bungalow and was so di the first day or two nobody would play with her. By the second d name which made her furious.

It was Basil who thought of it first. Basil was a little boy with imp turned-up nose, and Mary hated him. She was playing by herself u been playing the day the cholera broke out. She was making heap garden and Basil came and stood near to watch her. Presently he g denly made a suggestion.

"Why don't you put a heap of stones there and pretend it is a roc middle," and he leaned over her to point.

"Go away!" cried Mary. "I don't want boys. Go away!"

For a moment Basil looked angry, and then he began to tease. He He danced round and round her and made faces and sang and lau

　　"Mistress Mary, quite contrary,
　　How does your garden grow?
　　With silver bells, and cockle shells,
　　And marigolds all in a row."

He sang it until the other children heard and laughed, too; and th they sang "Mistress Mary, quite contrary"; and after that as long as called her "Mistress Mary Quite Contrary" when they spoke of h when they spoke to her.

mother of two

born in 1849

oldest son died young

British-American
Caucasian
published in 1911

Create a Question

We want students to be able to answer high level questions, but we also want them to create these types of questions. If your students need a little help doing this, try using a Create A Question bag.

I developed question stems from the top three levels of Bloom's Taxonomy. These are generic enough that they can be used with almost any content. Then I cut them up and placed some into each of several bags. Each team was given a bag and every student was to reach in and select a question. They had a few minutes to generate a question based on our lesson, write it down on a blank strip of paper and place it into the teacher's bag.

Original stem:

What type of people would be on your team to solve ...

became:

What type of people would be on your team to solve the energy crisis?

We then randomly chose student questions to read aloud and answer. Students were highly engaged and excited to answer their peers' questions. Simple and reusable!

Create a Question

What is the function of

What does the author believe about

What's the relationship between

How is this similar to

What are some of the problems of

What is the difference between

Are there any inconsistencies

Is there a better solution to

How effective are

continued—

Reproducible 68: Create a Question, continued

What are some of the consequences of

How does this influence

What are the pros and cons of

If you had unlimited resources, how would you

What might be a new way to

What might be an unusual way to combine

How would you test or check

What would the solution

What type of people would be on your team to solve

Four Card Vocab Concentration

Ready to mix things up a bit for your students? Try this Four Card Concentration strategy for practicing vocabulary. All you need for this strategy are four index cards per word. If you want to make it a bit easier, use a different color for each of the four tasks. Have the students create cards for their essential vocabulary terms.

1. Word (green)

2. Definition (yellow)

3. Synonym (orange)

4. Illustration (pink)

After creating cards for each term, mix them up and place them on the floor (face up—easier, or face down—harder.) Match the cards, two at a time. Any two of the four can be a match, i.e., definition and illustration. Try it yourself with these seventh grade science cards in the image!

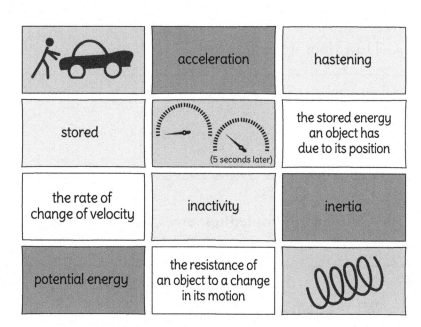

State and Restate

I was working with a creative group of teachers from American Leadership Academy in Arizona. The teaching ideas were being generated so quickly that the temperature rose to 116 degrees! I challenged the group to develop variations on the traditional "ticket out the door" idea. Here's one of the ideas a teacher shared.

1. Give the students a paper that has the outline of your state, repeated twice, like the example shown Better yet, save the prep time and just have students draw it.

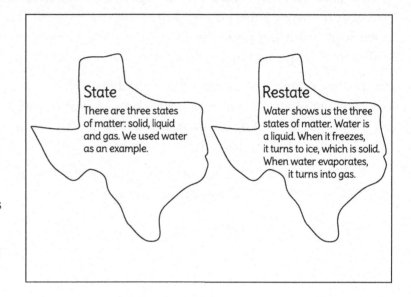

State

There are three states of matter: solid, liquid and gas. We used water as an example.

Restate

Water shows us the three states of matter. Water is a liquid. When it freezes, it turns to ice, which is solid. When water evaporates, it turns into gas.

2. Have them label the left as *State* and the right as *Restate*.

3. Direct students to "state" what they learned in the lesson, and then paraphrase or "restate" what they learned.

Memory experts tell us that students need to recode learning into their own words in order to move it into long-term memory. This is such a simple way to do that! I especially love that it can be used by any teacher, any subject area, any grade level!

Learning Journey

A Learning Journey is a wonderful way to capture learning over time or throughout a unit of instruction. Because research supports the use of non-linguistic approaches to capture and review concepts, I have used this strategy with students in the past. I have also used it with adults in my workshops. During a three day professional learning class on co-teaching, we documented our learning with words and pictures on a scroll of chart paper hung on the wall. I love no-prep strategies like this one!

Simply hang a piece of butcher paper on a wall. Draw a long, curvy road from one end of the paper to the other. Throughout your lesson or unit, ask students to go to the wall with colored markers and add illustrations and words that represent their learning so far. At the end of your lesson or unit, go back to the journey for a quick, visual review.

➲ Students can keep track of their own learning journeys by drawing a road on a piece of paper or in a notebook and illustrating as they travel with you through the unit.

Prior Knowledge Spinners

Activating prior knowledge is a common educational phrase. Almost any teacher will tell you the importance of getting students to make connections to their background knowledge before they learn about a new topic or read a new story.

Recently I searched for ideas on how to activate prior knowledge. Everything I found included the teacher doing the activating of the students—an external event, rather than students learning how to activate their own brains. We need our students to be able to do this independently! During standardized assessments, teachers are not able to prompt students with questions, K–W–L charts, and other hints about the topic. During most authentic learning situations, I don't have someone saying to me, "What do you Know about this topic?"

So how does one activate one's own knowledge? What do you do when faced with a topic you know little about? I reflected on my own experience and then developed a tool to help my students. The Prior Knowledge Spinner (see **Reproducible 72a**) provides six questions to stimulate metacognition, particularly as it relates to prior knowledge. I provided students with the topic, then had them spin and answer the questions.

I also created a second version with visual prompts to help our English learners or other students who needed some additional support (see **Reproducible 72b**).

Our goal is to have students use the spinners frequently enough that the questions become embedded in their metacognitive processes. This will include a transition phase when we fade out the actual spinners and encourage a visualization.

Prior Knowledge Spinners

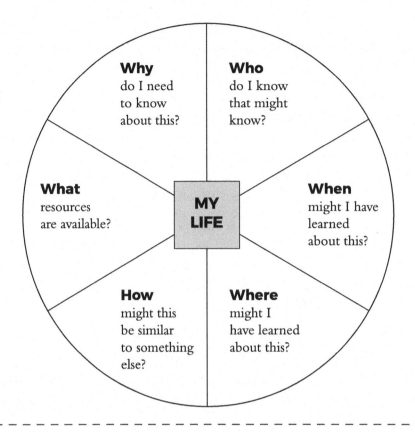

Prior Knowledge Spinners

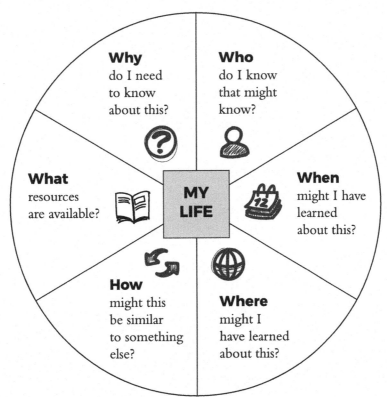

Pattern Search

Sandra Kaplan, a researcher in California, has identified eleven areas of depth and complexity that teachers can add to their instruction. One of these areas is patterns. There are patterns in just about everything, but we often don't notice them. Patterns can help us make sense of things and lead us to new ideas.

Here's a simple way to help students become more aware of patterns. Photocopy **Reproducible 73**, cut along the dotted lines and hand it to students who are ready for a challenge or have finished their work early. Ask them to share their thinking with you or with the class.

Pattern Search

Pattern Search

Patterns exist in everything. Sometimes they are very obvious, other times very subtle. Can you find any patterns in today's lesson content?

Pattern Search

Patterns exist in everything. Sometimes they are very obvious, other times very subtle. Can you find any patterns in today's lesson content?

Pattern Search

Patterns exist in everything. Sometimes they are very obvious, other times very subtle. Can you find any patterns in today's lesson content?

Pattern Search

Patterns exist in everything. Sometimes they are very obvious, other times very subtle. Can you find any patterns in today's lesson content?

Question the Text

Years ago I read an article by Alfie Kohn in which he claimed that teachers were ruining students' abilities to think critically. He wrote that the educators tend to prefer students who are compliant (very true) and that by demanding compliance from students, we were squashing their natural inclination to question things.

While I didn't fully agree with him, it did get me questioning my own practices. Was there a way that I could encourage students to challenge authority in a respectful, appropriate way?

Out of that reflection grew my Challenge Authority Cards (see **Reproducible 13**). While I have developed a variety of them, I particularly like these that ask students to challenge or question the text they are reading. This skill is especially important as students read information on unscreened internet sources.

I find this is a great way to engage some of the higher level thinkers in a class—or early finishers. If you keep these handy, you can use them on the spur of the moment. So, just copy the following reproducible, cut them up and hand them to students who are ready for a challenge.

Tip

➡ For more questions, check out **Super Strategy 13: Challenge Authority Cards**.

Question the Text

Question the text. Did the author(s) make any errors? What makes you think so?

Question the text. Did the author(s) use any poor examples? What would you replace?

Question the text. Did the author(s) have a biased perspective? What makes you think so?

Question the text. Did the author(s) leave out something essential? What would you include?

Question the text. Does the fact that the text was written more than five years ago affect the information? If so, how?

Question the text. What societal pressures might have affected the way the author(s) portrayed this topic?

Question the text. How could the author(s) have made this more appealing to students?

Stop for Popcorn

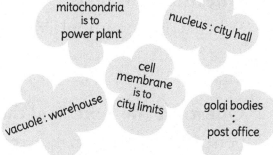

Video is a wonderful media for engaging students and providing them close to real-life experiences. However, its effectiveness is maximized if students are given a viewing purpose and a concrete way to capture their ideas.

Try the Stop for Popcorn Strategy. I took yellow sticky notes and cut them to look (a bit) like popcorn. We gave each student one and explained that when you go to the movies, you take time out to munch on popcorn—just like we could stop during the video to make a note on our popcorn stickies.

A specific prompt was provided on the board. In this biology class, we wanted to students to complete an analogy based on ideas in the video, so the prompt was:

cell : city

_____ : _____

After viewing the video students came up to the board and placed their popcorn, on which they had written an analogy, in a large popcorn tub that I had drawn. Discussion followed.

Formative Assessment Face

In Shakespeare's *Macbeth*, King Duncan says, "There's no art to find the mind's construction in the face." While the meaning here is that the human face can hide all types of treachery, perhaps an innovative teacher can use student faces to gather accurate information!

Try this idea that I picked up from a creative teacher.

1. Give each student a paper plate and a writing utensil.

2. On your screen, present four or five multiple choice questions, one at a time. The question can have two to four choices, but each choice will be linked with a shape. For example:

"Students should be able to use cell phones in school."

    yes = use triangles for eyes

    no = use ovals for eyes

"I know all I need to know about internet security."

    yes = use a square for a nose

    no = use a pentagon for a nose

These types of questions would lead to the development of an opinion face. You can also design content review questions such as:

"Which of the following is not necessary for growing plants?"

    sunlight = use suns for eyes

    water = use tear drops for eyes

    salt = use a square for eyes

    nutrients = use ovals for eyes

As the students are drawing their faces, the teacher can wander the room glancing at their creations and gathering formative assessment data.

As an alternative, students can draw on whiteboards or paper.

Learning Bands

Athletic teams and charitable groups have used wrist bands for several years as a way to promote their organizations and goals. Frequently, students can be seen with several different colored bands dangling around their wrists. Here's an idea for tapping into this interest to promote your learning goals, especially with rote information such as spelling words and math facts. (Great for primary grade students!)

Obtain two different colors of Velcro® (the non–adhesive type). From one color, cut strips approximately seven inches in length. On the other color, use a permanent marker to write numbers and operational signs (or letters for spelling.) The written material will attach to the wristband strips, so be sure to use the opposite Velcro structures so that they will stick together. Finally, cut a one inch piece to serve as a clasp or connecting device to hold the band together.

At the start of the day direct your students to create a band that shows one of the math facts that they have not yet mastered (or to spell their name, or phone number, or missed spelling word). As they wear the learning bands throughout the day they will see a frequent reminder of the key fact they need to learn!

Analogy Tower

Analogies are a creative way to show higher level thinking. To make the process a bit more concrete and engaging, try building Lego® or Duplo® towers.

The lesson objective for this day was about the differences between narrative and essay writing. After a mini-lesson in which we generated a T-chart and analyzed samples, a quick formative assessment told us which students grasped the concept thoroughly and could engage in enrichment.

Students in the enrichment group were given a bag of Lego or Duplo blocks and a water-based marker. A laminated direction sheet was included in the bag so that the activity could be self-directed. (The analogy prompt on the direction sheet can be changed to fit the lesson content.)

The directions provided students with the first part of the analogy …

narrative is to *essay*

… and they had to complete the analogy on the blocks as they built a tower. I was impressed with their creativity and grasp of the concept! Students were engaged with higher level thinking skills and enjoying themselves.

Perhaps the best part is that this bag can be kept in the classroom and pulled out at any time we feel that some students need a challenge. All the teacher will need to do is provide the first part of the analogy. Examples might include *sun* is to *food web*; *vertex* is to *angle*; *democracy* is to *communism*; *adjective* is to *noun*.

Analogy Tower

Directions

You will be building an analogy tower similar to the one below.

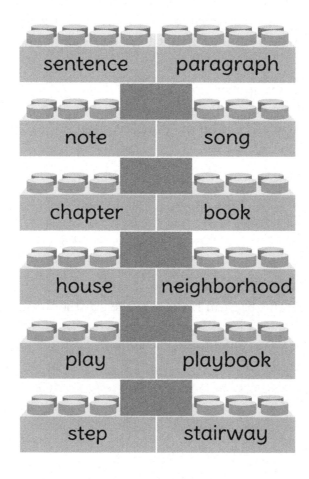

Start with: _____ is to _____

1. Think about what makes the relationship between these two words unique.

2. Think of other pairs of words that have a similar relationship.

3. Write them on the blocks.

Letter Bag

A teacher in Delaware showed me this simple strategy for engaging students. The teacher had ten paper lunch bags, one for each small group to share. Inside the bags she had placed 26 cards, each with one letter of the alphabet. The lesson objective was to identify and discuss the impact of the narrative elements in a story. Students were listening to the teacher read, and reading along in their own books. Every so often, the teacher stopped, directed the students to pull a letter out of their "letter bag," and then make a connection between the letter and a narrative element. For example, one group pulled an "O" and discussed how the setting of the story was "outdoors." Another group pulled an "E" and wondered what the "exciting" climax would be.

This is the type of strategy I love for three reasons:

1. Highly engaging—it was multi-modality and had an element of unpredictability that students immediately loved.

2. Highly applicable—the same strategy could be used to encourage connections to any content discussion, as an activator, or even as a summarizing moment, K–12!

3. Low prep—such a quick thing to put together.

Word Toss

Many teachers use the Frayer Model (1969) as a vocabulary application activity. The Frayer Model typically involves asking students to fold or divide their paper into four sections. In one quadrant the students write the word and definition, in another they write facts/characteristics, in another quadrant examples, and finally non-examples.

To mix things up a bit, try replacing your Frayer Model with a Word Toss activity. We placed students into pairs and provided each pair with a die and a Word Toss worksheet. Students were directed to role the dice and perform the task associated with the number on the face of their die.

The change in routine increased alertness by adding some novelty and tactile interaction to the lesson. Afterward, my co-teacher and I brainstormed alternative tasks that could go on the Word Toss worksheet:

- Act it out
- Develop a metaphor
- Develop an analogy
- Create a multiple choice question
- Perform word surgery (dissect into root, prefix, suffix)
- Transform it (add prefix or suffix)
- Career Track it (think of a job for which you would need this word)
- Create a crossword clue

Word Toss

Non-Example

Sentence

Synonym

Antonym

Description

Draw It

Tickets Out the Door

Educational experts suggest that each lesson should have a closure activity—something that wraps up the experience or gives students a chance to summarize their learning. Many teachers have chosen to use a Ticket Out the Door activity for closure and as a formative assessment. This is an easy, multi-purpose strategy that can be used with almost any content or grade level.

However, Tickets Out the Door can lose their effectiveness with students if they are overdone. To avoid this problem, consider adding some variety to your tickets! The prompts below can be displayed on the board, reinforced with a printed visual on a ticket, or students can quickly draw the related shape on a scrap of paper.

Tickets Out the Door

If you were to fill a grocery cart with key concepts from today's lesson, what would it contain?

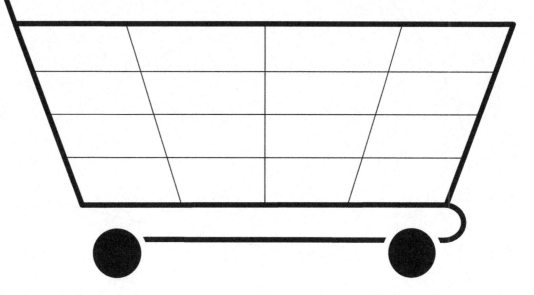

- -

If you were to fill a grocery cart with key concepts from today's lesson, what would it contain?

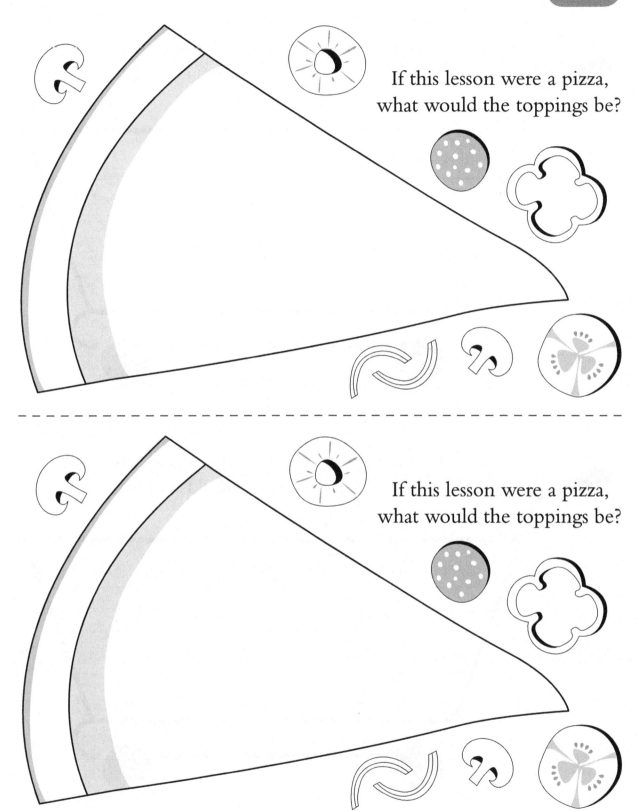

If this lesson were a pizza, what would the toppings be?

If this lesson were a pizza, what would the toppings be?

Tickets Out the Door

Write a news headline based on what you learned today.

THE DAILY NEWS

TODAY'S HEADLINE:

_____

_____

Write a news headline based on what you learned today.

THE DAILY NEWS

TODAY'S HEADLINE:

_____

_____

Write a news headline based on what you learned today.

THE DAILY NEWS

TODAY'S HEADLINE:

_____

_____

Tickets Out the Door

What new learning will you
walk away with today?

_____
_____
_____
_____

What new learning will you
walk away with today?

_____
_____
_____
_____

What new learning will you
walk away with today?

_____
_____
_____
_____

Write a recipe for _____.

🥄 My Recipe 🥄

_____

_____

_____

_____

_____

_____

_____

_____

- -

Write a recipe for _____.

🥄 My Recipe 🥄

_____

_____

_____

_____

_____

_____

_____

_____

Tickets Out the Door

Write a text message summary of what you learned today.

Write a text message summary of what you learned today.

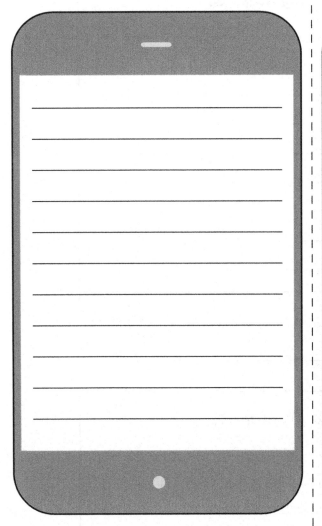

Tickets Out the Door

How can you make money from what you learned today?

- -

How can you make money from what you learned today?

Tickets Out the Door

If this concept were turned into a menu,
what would be the appetizer? Main dish? Dessert?

∾ M E N U ∾

☕ **Appetizer** _____

_____

🍽 **Main Dish** _____

_____

_____

🧁 **Dessert** _____

_____

- -

If this concept were turned into a menu,
what would be the appetizer? Main dish? Dessert?

∾ M E N U ∾

☕ **Appetizer** _____

_____

🍽 **Main Dish** _____

_____

_____

🧁 **Dessert** _____

_____

Tickets Out the Door

Complete an analogy, beginning with today's concept.

_____ is to _____

as

_____ is to _____

- -

Complete an analogy, beginning with today's concept.

_____ is to _____

as

_____ is to _____

- -

Complete an analogy, beginning with today's concept.

_____ is to _____

as

_____ is to _____

Tickets Out the Door

Write a postcard to a friend or family member
explaining what you did in class today.

Write a postcard to a friend or family member
explaining what you did in class today.

Scratch Off Review ▰▰▰▰

Everyone in my household found a scratch-off lottery ticket in their Christmas stocking this year. We each experienced a few moments of hope and excitement as we carefully chose the spots to scratch. You can add that same fun to your classroom instruction with scratch-off stickers. These are available from several websites and are fairly inexpensive. Just print out a list of review items—events, dates, vocabulary—and place a sticker over each item. You can also simulate the experience even less expensively by laminating your review list and dabbing a bit of poster paint over each item. When the paint dries it can be scratched off with a coin, revealing the item underneath.

I have used this strategy in many classes, including a middle school science class. Each student wrote a prediction about the outcome of an experiment, then covered over their prediction with a scratch-off sticker. After the experiment, students swapped with a peer and scratched off to see if the predictions were correct.

For digital versions of the reproducibles in this book,
go to https://tinyurl.com/yx52trth.

The reproducibles can also be found
on Anne's website at
www.ideasforeducators.com/downloadables.html.

Notes

Notes

Notes

Notes

Notes

Notes

References

Boykin, A., K. Tyler, K. Watkins-Lewis, and K. Kizzie. 2006. Culture in the sanctioned classroom practices of elementary school teachers serving low-income African American students. *Journal of Education for Students Placed at Risk* 11: 161–173.

Bradbury, R. 1953. *Fahrenheit 451.* New York: Ballantine.

Burnett, F. H. and T. Tudor. 1962. *The secret garden.* Philadelphia: J.B. Lippincott Company.

Cooper, C. R. and L. Odell, ed. 1999. *Evaluating writing: The role of teachers' knowledge about text, learning, and culture.* Urbana, IL: National Council of Teachers of English.

Frayer, D., W. C. Frederick, and H. J. Klausmeier. 1969. *A schema for testing the level of cognitive mastery.* Madison, WI: Wisconsin Center for Education Research.

Gregory, G. and M. Kaufeldt. 2015. *The motivated brain: Improving student attention, engagement and perseverance.* Alexandria, VA: Association for Supervision and Curriculum Development.

Hughes, C. and S. Asakawa. "Keep calm and doodle on." Nova Education (blog). 2014. http://www.pbs.org/wgbh/nova/blogs/education/2014/07/keep-calm-and-doodle-on.

Joossee, B. M. 1996. *I love you the purplest.* San Fransisco: Chronicle Books, 148.

Kohn, A. "Choices for children: Why and how to let students decide." *Phi Delta Kappan* (September 1993). http://www.alfiekohn.org/article/choices-children.

Payne, R. 2008. Nine powerful practices. *Educational Leadership* 65 (7): 48–52.

Polacco, P. 1988. *The keeping quilt.* New York: Simon & Schuster.

Wilhelm, J. 2002. *Action strategies for deepening comprehension.* New York: Scholastic.

Made in United States
Orlando, FL
01 July 2022

19319829R00109